MW01012312

LOOKING AT THE
LIGHTS

LOOKING AT THE LIGHTS

MY PATH FROM FAN TO A WRESTLING HEEL

PETE GAS
WITH JON ROBINSON

Forewords by Adam "Edge" Copeland
and
John Bradshaw Layfield

SPORTS
PUBLISHING

Copyright © 2017 by Pete Gas with Jon Robinson
Foreword copyright © 2017 by Adam Copeland
Foreword copyright © 2017 by John Bradshaw Layfield

All rights reserved. No part of this book may be reproduced in any manner without the express written consent of the publisher, except in the case of brief excerpts in critical reviews or articles. All inquiries should be addressed to Sports Publishing, 307 West 36th Street, 11th Floor, New York, NY 10018.

Sports Publishing books may be purchased in bulk at special discounts for sales promotion, corporate gifts, fund-raising, or educational purposes. Special editions can also be created to specifications. For details, contact the Special Sales Department, Sports Publishing, 307 West 36th Street, 11th Floor, New York, NY 10018 or sportspubbooks@skyhorsepublishing.com.

Sports Publishing® is a registered trademark of Skyhorse Publishing, Inc.®, a Delaware corporation.

Visit our website at www.sportspubbooks.com.

10 9 8 7 6 5 4 3 2 1

Library of Congress Cataloging-in-Publication Data is available on file.

Cover design by Tom Lau
Cover photograph courtesy of World Wrestling Entertainment, Inc.

Photos in insert (where noted) are courtesy of World Wrestling Entertainment, Inc.

Print ISBN: 978-1-61321-987-4
Ebook ISBN: 978-1-61321-988-1

Printed in the United States of America

This book is dedicated to the memory of my father.
The late, great, and original Pete Gas.

You'll always be in my heart.

TABLE OF CONTENTS

Foreword by

Adam "Edge" Copeland

The year was 1999. Limp Bizkit was still atop the charts. Everyone was doing it for the "Nookie." *Titanic* was becoming the highest grossing film of all time (more on the film's visionary director later). Rubber Goth choker necklaces were actually an acceptable fashion accessory. It was an era when tramp stamps were considered a good idea. Tribal tattoos were all the rage, and Rage Against the Machine were at their full, angry, groove-laden power. Alas, it was also a year when two young, lion maned, Hot Topic–wearing kids from the burbs of Toronto finally found themselves realizing their dreams of competing in the WWE. A squinty-eyed fucker named Jay Reso (a.k.a. Christian) and myself were trying to knock the tag team world—along with The Hardy Boyz and eventually the Dudley Boyz (notice the z, like I said: 1999)—on its butt.

Around the same time, and a little less remembered, was the debut of three dudes from the mean streets of Greenwich, Connecticut (although one member, Joey Abs, was from the woods of North Carolina). They were Rodney Leinhardt, the aforementioned indie veteran Abs, and Pete Gasparino (a.k.a. Pete Gas). The Mean Street Posse. Clad in sweater vests and chinos (but strangely, wrestling boots), they looked like those guys in high school you either wanted to hang out with or really DIDN'T want to hang out with. They were the Socs from *The Outsiders.* The Ralph Lauren–loving lacrosse players who'd eventually find themselves in Ivy League schools and sweet-paying jobs as CEOs.

Pete and Rod were actually childhood friends of Shane McMahon. They were brought in to play back-up for Shane in his big WrestleMania match with X-Pac. I don't think they quite understood what they were in for. On paper, you say, "hey, talk about a dream gig!" There's plenty of wrestlers out there who would give their eye teeth, their nose teeth, and their ear teeth for that opportunity. Yes I know there's no such thing as nose and ear teeth, I'm a storyteller. Forgive my long, mostly useless analogies.

A wrestling locker room can be an unforgiving, uncompromising, unwelcoming place. Take any "un" you want, and that locker room was it. Like a stalactite-ridden cave with a hibernating Grizzly snoring in its cold, wet confines. Picture a shark tank full of sinewy 20-foot great whites, and throw in some hungry alpha wolves who are really good swimmers and that should give you an idea. That's if you can actually wrestle and aren't friends with the owner's son. Well they WERE Shane's friends, and make no mistake about it: the Posse COULDN'T wrestle. At first. Abs was added so they could have some experience to get them through matches on their end. They were thrown in the deep end. The deepest part of the ocean deep. Where the Kraken lives. Where half of James Cameron's movies take place type deep (and there's your callback). The match at WrestleMania was their initial, pardon the pun, test.

For me and Christian, we always liked the Posse and understood the tough position they were in. Plus we were roughly the same age, were also buddies with Shane and, most importantly, they were just good dudes. So we took every chance we could to give them advice. We even got to work each other and they knew they could be comfortable with us. We "managed" them against the Hardy's with the proviso that if they won, we got the first title shot. We were conniving Canadians. Good times. And here's the thing with Pete: amidst all of the beatings at the hands of the APA and assorted other grizzled long-time veterans, he never complained once. Better yet, I never saw the guy not smiling. He clearly understood what was happening but instead of developing a chip on his shoulder, he chose to develop skills.

Imagine, if you will, being thrown into the NFL having never played one down of football, lining up against Ray Lewis. That's the equivalent of what Pete faced when he stepped in the ring with someone like Ron Simmons. At that point a 13-year veteran who just happened to be the first African American World Champion in history and can bench press a Volkswagen while wearing jeans and cowboy boots with his daily paper tucked under his arm. Yeah, that put it in perspective, right? But Pete never complained. Never griped, never bitched or moaned. He just laughed and smiled. Which was the absolute best thing he could have done. He paid his dues. He worked hard. He got better.

xii   LOOKING AT THE LIGHTS

Sometimes in business that doesn't matter though. In the WWE there's generally a yearly roster thinning. In 2001, it was Pete's turn to be cut. At the time he was in Puerto Rico, where he was sent to continue honing his skills. This was after he had been sent to Memphis, with the idea of possibly going to Japan. He wanted to get better. However, even in the midst of all of this and being released, he didn't get bitter.

That was my memory of Pete. Over the years we'd see each other, but pretty rarely. In one of the instances that social media isn't annoying, Pete and I got back in contact through Twitter. When Christian and I started filming our show, *The Edge and Christian Show that Totally Reeks of Awesomeness* for the WWE Network, Pete was one of the first people we asked to be on. He plays the mailman. As Pete Gas. To deliver Paul Heyman's cut-off pony tail. While also mimicking Kevin Spacey from *7even*. No, it doesn't make sense, but nothing on our show does. So deal with it. Best part is that all these years later, Pete was the same guy. Smiling, laughing, and happy to be on the show. Oh yeah, and he killed it too.

Pete didn't let a sometimes bloodthirsty industry change him. He moved on.

So while you read this and reminisce about your lost 90s weekends and look regretfully in the mirror at your lower back where your tribal butterfly tattoo lives, now looking like a melting moth, while listening to Fred Durst, just know that Pete Gas is in a good place. There, feel better? I kid, I kid. Really what this is, is a feel good story about a good time, a good guy, who hasn't changed. And sometimes that's enough, isn't it?

—Adam "Edge" Copeland

Foreword by

John Bradshaw Layfield

You never know in wrestling what will work—we wish it was so easy. If someone had told us that you could take three guys off the street and put them in the ring and they would be successful, we would have laughed . . . but that is exactly what happened with Pete Gas and his Mean Street Posse.

Most people who had made it into the WWE had been many places and spent many years learning the business. In my case, which is typical, I had wrestled all over the world: I had lived in Europe for a couple of years wrestling every night after starting in Texas and Japan. Nearly everyone who was in the WWE had been a champion somewhere in a smaller territory/regional promotion. It is similar to professional sports that you get your players by choosing the best out of college or in rare instances high school; however, no one goes straight to the pros without at least playing the game.

The fact that Pete Gas and his Mean Street Posse went straight to the top and actually made it as stars is mind blowing to say the least.

Being a villain in professional wrestling is the best. Who doesn't want to punch the big bully who does nothing but brag, or who doesn't want to shut up a bunch of rich kids from Greenwich who think they are tough? Without a good villain, the white knight never gets to ride in and save the day.

The idea of Mean Street Posse is absurd—thugs from the mean streets of Greenwich—where the toughest thing you had to worry about was whether your chauffeur picked you up from your preppy boarding school. At least that's the characters these guys played, and I loved it. In fact, I thought it was genius.

I remember, during one of our matches, hitting Pete so hard with a metal chair that it just folded around his head. After the match we got to the back and he just laughed. That's just how we played it back then. We took pride in making things look real. When I say that pro wrestling is like the circus I don't do it justice, we were much crazier than the circus.

We used to wreck into each other like crash-up derby in rental cars going down the road, we were constantly playing jokes on each other (we called ribs), and we loved the night life. We were overgrown kids having the time of our lives . . . the business has since changed now just like the NFL has, but when Pete was in the WWE he was a part of the "good old days."

The boss's son brought Pete into the WWE, something that in most instances would have been a political nightmare. But not with Pete. We all loved Shane McMahon and when he brought his friends in with him, they fit in just like guys who had been in the business for years.

We have an incredibly respectful business and Pete never had any issues, and that really says something about him as a person. I share something with Pete that everyone in the history of the business would be jealous of: the highest rated regular quarter hour in wrestling history. Pete and his boys were fighting the "Stooges" of Pat Patterson and Gerald Brisco and in the same quarter hour I was fighting my tag team partner Ron Simmons. We did an astounding 8.6 rating. Imagine taking a guy off the street and drawing a rating like that?

The problem that Pete had was he was too entertaining. People like to be entertained and, when a character entertains people, even if that character is the bad guy, eventually the crowd turns them into a fan favorite. This happened to Pete—he was just too entertaining, which is a good thing.

Pete has a great story. He came to WWE to do a simple storyline and because of his ability he not only stayed, he became a star.

—John Bradshaw Layfield

Introduction

You never forget the first time you get whacked in the head by a steel chair.

Then again, that's just the life of a professional wrestler, especially during the era I performed, the only era people seem to want to talk about these days, as it's an era packed with more shocks, more laughs, and more characters than arguably any other era in the business. I was a product of that era, WWE's "Attitude Era," performing as a wrestler who I hope you loved to hate. It was my job to get you so mad that you'd want to spit on me, cuss at me, and cheer when I got my bell rung by legends like the Rock, Stone Cold Steve Austin, and JBL.

And getting your bell rung is just one of the ways you had to earn respect from the other wrestlers in that locker room.

That's why I hate when people call professional wrestling fake. Scripted? Fine. Choreographed chaos/violence? Of course. But believe me, the cuts, the broken bones, the blood dripping on the mat, that's all too real, and I still have the sore neck and loss of memory to prove it. You just can't fake falling through a table or taking a bump outside the ring on concrete. I read a study a long time ago that said being in a wrestling match is the equivalent of your body going through thirty car accidents. When you land on concrete, your body stops, but everything inside moves around, and it's that jarring which really causes the pain.

But when you're in the ring, when you're in that moment, the adrenaline is flowing and you're not thinking about how much pain you're in. You're just trying to put on the best match, the best show you possibly can. You think about it when you get back to your hotel room, when you need to fill the ice bucket so you can take care of all the bumps and bruises, that's when you feel it. That's when you realize what you just put your body through. But unless you break a bone or blow out your quad like Triple H did, you keep going. You owe it to the fans, to the guys you're in the ring with, and the guys watching from the locker room. It's up to you to work through the pain.

It's funny, because anyone who doesn't believe me, anyone who thinks the chair shots don't hurt or the bouncy ring mat saves our bodies, all you have to do is turn on the WWE Network and go watch the episode of *Monday Night Raw* where the Mean Street Posse took on the Acolytes. JBL hit me with a chair shot so devastating that it actually wrapped around my head like an old *Flintstones* cartoon. At times I wonder if the WWE actually had the video taken down off of YouTube because the hit was so violent. I actually just watched this match and, when you look at the video, the referee Teddy Long was in the corner, he actually covers his face the chair shot was so bad. And people always want to know what it feels like to get blasted in the skull by a steel chair. Let me tell you, every single time I got hit in the head, I saw a big flash of light and my ears would immediately start to ring. But I never saw a bigger flash or was more disorientated than the night of Bradshaw's hit.

To put it bluntly, Bradshaw hit me so hard in the head that Mick Foley was worried about my health.

That's right, Mick Foley, the guy who got thrown off the top of the Hell in a Cell cage and then was choke slammed through the roof of it so hard his tooth ended up in his nose. *He* thought the chair shot was too extreme.

The following day, we took a charter flight to Tallahassee, Florida. I remember Mick Foley pulling me aside and asking, "Are you OK?" He was like, "Pete, I've taken many chair shots to the head and that was a bad one." He couldn't believe that I was able to even get up after the match.

But I was like, "Yeah, I'm fine, no big deal."

Later, Chris Jericho pulled me aside and told me he'd never seen anything like that. He told me: "Don't lie to me, are you OK?"

I told him I was fine, but then he tells me: "Well, you're probably facing the Acolytes again tonight. Do yourself a favor, feed him your back. You don't want to take another one of those chair shots to the head. That was brutal."

But when the Mean Street Posse debuted in the WWE, we were the new guys, we had no wrestling experience, no training, but there we were, on the most talked about wrestling show on the planet, and that was just one of the ways you paid your dues in the WWE. We didn't put our hands up for chair shots. We needed to prove we were tough. We needed to prove we could take it and come back for more. We were there to show everyone that we could compete with the best of them, and if that meant taking a wicked chair shot to prove it, that's just the price we paid for our shot at being superstars.

The Mean Street Posse might not have been the most gifted athletes in the ring, but one thing you could never take away from us was our toughness and desire to be there.

Chapter 1

Mean Street Wasn't Actually Paved in Gold

The funniest thing about being in the Mean Street Posse is that everyone I meet assumes I'm a millionaire. Not as a kid, not now, never was. Couldn't be further from the truth. Only thing about the Mean Street storyline that was true was the fact that Rodney and I had been close friends with Shane long before we ever wore preppy sweaters on *Monday Night Raw*.

Growing up, there were three different junior high schools in Greenwich, Connecticut. Rodney and Shane went to Central Middle School and I went to Eastern Middle School. When we faced them in football, I played both ways (offense and defense) and remember facing Shane head-on at the line of scrimmage plenty of times. And boy was that kid tough, even back then. I knew of him and his family, and, of course, I had been watching wrestling since I was nine; staying up late to watch Hulk Hogan, King Kong Bundy, and Andre the Giant. So I knew who the kid was, and I too stereotyped him. But since he was on the other team, we weren't friends. I was taught in football that the only friends you have are the guys on your team. Everyone else is your enemy. But that all changed when we were in high school. By the time we got to the tenth grade, we all ended up on the same team, and now my enemy was about to become one of my best friends for life.

Shane and I were both on the offensive line together with Rodney as the fullback, and we instantly hit it off. It's funny, because I think a lot of people's first impression of Shane is that he comes off a little pompous because of all the money he grew up around. But in all honesty, the more you get to know him, the more you realize that he isn't like that at all. However, the more you get to know him, the more you realize he's absolutely crazy (and I mean that in the best kind of way). The kid is an adrenaline junkie, he seriously has no fear. I remember we used to hang out at this dam in Greenwich, and nobody knew how deep the water was, but that didn't stop Shane one day from climbing to the top. We were all laughing like, "No way he's going to jump." But he just looked at us, and next thing you know he takes off without hesitation, jumping off the top and splashing into the water below. As he was falling, all I could think was, "Shane's dead," but damn if he didn't swim right back to the top of the water and let out a scream of conquest. He was a risk-taker for sure. If Shane saw something high up in the air, his first comment was always about wanting to jump off of it. He wouldn't think twice, he'd just do it and somehow always ended up smelling like a rose (sound familiar, Undertaker?).

Being around Shane is always fun, always entertaining. I like to tell him: I've never had a bad time hanging out with you. Whenever we went out, we always had a fun night. It wasn't about money either. We all made our own money working various jobs and would honestly get upset if he disappeared and paid the check before we even saw it. To be honest, some of the best nights we ever spent together had nothing to do with money at all. There's just something about Shane that brings out the madman in everyone who's around him. Even if we were getting chased by the cops or acting reckless, it was always a blast. I remember one time when we were freshmen in college, Shane decided it would be a blast to take the McMahon's maid's car out for a joy ride. It was a metallic green, ugly freakin' Lincoln Town Car. Shane wanted to take it out that night because his pickup was in the shop (again), plus the Lincoln was so huge that he could fit everyone in one car. We were all at a party and I was trying to talk to a girl, but Shane and a group of our friends were all bored and wanted to leave and go to a bar. So he gets three other guys and they each grab one of my limbs, pick me up, and carry me to the car. We all had fake IDs at the time thanks to one of the other offensive linemen on our team who would make them in his basement senior year, and these IDs always worked, so we always wanted to hop around the bar scene. I obviously had no say in the matter.

So Shane starts driving and Rodney and Willie Green (who was actually in one of the original Mean Street Posse vignettes, but never wrestled) decide that they are going to climb onto the roof of the car while Shane is doing about 80 down the highway. I'm serious: if you knew our crew, we were doing stuff from *Jackass* before *Jackass* even existed. It's just what we did. These two guys jump out on the roof, then Rodney decides to move from the roof to sliding his way down the hood of the car, hanging on by the windshield wipers. He was wearing a button down shirt with a pocket in the front, and that's where he always kept his can of tobacco. So Rodney decides that it's time for a chew, and he's going to grab the can and take a dip while riding on the hood. But the fool drops the can and it slowly starts to slide toward the end of the hood as we continue to book it down the road. This is when Rodney's brain needed to decide: What's more important, your life or your tobacco? Of course, Rodney went with the tobacco. He didn't want to part with it. So he actually takes both hands off the wipers and hood, grabs the can of tobacco, then before falling to his death actually grabbed back on to the windshield wipers. He then continued to ride on the hood for a good five miles. But that's not all. As Shane saw the boys having so much fun, he decided to not only join them but to top them. So Shane switches out from the driver's seat and tells me to drive. He then climbs on top of the car's roof while I floor it, and he's up there surfing the roof of this Town Car like he's Teen Wolf. It was one of the stupidest/funniest things I've ever seen. I can't believe none of us died that night, and we hadn't even made it to the bar yet.

After what seemed like hours of risking our lives for the thrill, we finally arrive in Port Chester. The bars there were open until 4 a.m., so that was always the go-to place-to-be for us and our fake IDs. Once we were there, the drinking was on and, in no time, Rodney meets up with a girl and she was good to go, so he gets up and immediately leaves with her. Rodney always had that ability with the ladies. So the rest of us all strike out, and now it's down to me, Willie Green, and Shane, and we hop back in the maid's Lincoln Town Car for the ride home.

Shane always preferred to drive through the back roads on our way back from Port Chester, but for some reason, playing Teen Wolf wasn't enough for him that night, so he decides he's going to start driving through people's bushes and crashing through sections of picket fences. He's just destroying everything in his path at this point, and we're all laughing and yelling, but when I turn around to look at the chaos we were leaving behind, I see a cop come flying up on our tail. Meanwhile, Willie Green has a rock about the size of a bowling ball and wants to throw it through someone's windshield. I yell, "Shane, there's a cop behind us," and he's like, "Psht, it's just a Jeep, don't worry about it."

Just a Jeep!? I know the difference between a Jeep's headlights and a cop's! So I yell, "There's a cop behind us!" But he still doesn't believe me and hits the gas even harder. That's when we saw the lights. Believe me now?

We'd been drinking, he'd been driving like a lunatic and smashing up half the neighborhood, and now the cop pulls us over and I know for sure we're all headed to jail. Willie throws the rock in my lap and tells me to cover it up. I put it on the floor and cover it with my feet, but I'm starting to sweat and Willie looks more like a guy trying to act cool than anything else. We were guilty as hell. But as soon as we get pulled over, Shane exits the vehicle to talk to the cop. Not a smart move. That's how you get shot. And that's when I hear this loud commotion and the cop starts to scream at Shane, and now I know we're all going down. I'm thinking my next time playing football is going to be on the prison team like *The Longest Yard*, and I just kept waiting for the cop to yell at us to get out with our hands up. But next thing I know, Shane gets back in the car and starts to drive away.

"Shane, how the fuck did you get out of this?" Apparently the cop was going to write Shane a ticket, and Shane asked if he could pay him cash to take care of the ticket on the spot. The cop was obviously offended by this and started shouting at Shane, and was about to put him in cuffs, but then when he read Shane's name again, he realized it was Vince McMahon's son, so everyone calmed down and he made us a deal that if Shane paid for all the damage he had done with his lunatic driving that we wouldn't be sent to jail. We all should've gotten arrested. The cop saw us taking out the fences and acting like idiots, but because Shane was a McMahon, we were all saved and I didn't have to join the prison football team after all.

* * *

When it comes to the McMahons, though, one thing people don't realize is this: despite all the drama you see on TV, they're one of the closest families I've ever met. Vince was a great dad and always there for his family. Shane and Vince were best friends when Shane was growing up. In fact, Vince was Shane's best man at his wedding. Vince was always there for him, whenever Shane needed him, and when Vince wasn't there, the McMahon name was sometimes all it took to get us out of trouble. But it was more than that. When we had our football games in high school, Vince would be at almost every game. I remember when we first got to high school, we'd be on the field and you'd look into the stands and there was Vince McMahon. You were so used to see-ing him on TV, but there he was watching his son's high school football game. I still remember the first time I got to meet him,

Vince shook my hand and all I could think was, "Holy shit, this guy is big!" He was into bodybuilding, even back then, and he had that wide back and big, bulky chest. The man was a beast. Still is.

It was always a blast hanging out at the McMahon house. Whether we were goofing around or even watching wrestling, it was the place to be for the guys to all get together and act like big-timers. Back then, Stephanie was still pretty young, but we all loved her like she was our little sister. When we were with Shane, Stephanie was always one of the guys. Nobody ever minded that Shane's little sister was hanging out with us because she was so cool. I remember when she was really little, all the guys over the house were sophomores and juniors in high school, and we were all talking about wrestling and what our wrestling names would be. I couldn't come up with a name, so I turn to Stephanie and I say, "Steph, if I was a wrestler, what would my name be?" And she looks at me, and she was so cute, and had this huge smile on her face as she says, "Flower." I was like, "What? What do you mean 'Flower?' What type of wrestler would go by the name Flower?" And she goes, "You would come out in all green and you could wear petals around your head. You would just be a big flower." It became a running joke with us, and when I see her to this day, we still call each other Flower. Out of all the tough and corny names everyone was coming up with, like Crusher and the Rhino, I became Flower.

Another fun thing we'd do at the McMahon's house was Casino Night. Shane used to invite everyone over, and we'd gamble on anything we could think of. We'd shoot pool for money, play poker or blackjack, and if you didn't know how to play those games, there were actually guys who'd play Go Fish for whatever amount of cash you wanted to throw down. We would have some beers and just go at it. Other times we'd be invited over and Vince would be there working on scripts for the following week's show. I even remember watching NFL playoff games in his living room. Vince is a big Washington Redskins fan, and I remember the year the Redskins were playing the Lions in the playoffs and we were all sitting in the living room watching, and Vince was just one of the guys screaming for his team and going wild when they scored a touchdown. It was great.

But there were times when Vince got mad. And when Vince got mad, to be honest, it scared the shit out of all of us. Back when we were juniors in high school, we had a buddy named Mike Cate, and Mike had a motorcycle. Like I said before, Shane was a daredevil, but the one thing Vince told him repeatedly not to do was hop on Mike's bike. Shane was forbidden from riding a motorcycle because Vince thought it was too dangerous a combination with Shane's stuntman self. One day, though, Shane decides that he can't stand it anymore, and he's going to ride the bike. He wasn't going to be stupid and ride it in front of his house. Instead, he goes a few blocks away where he thinks Vince won't see and starts to ride it around at high speeds like he's been riding motorcycles for years. I swear, the kid could pick up anything and look like an expert, and riding a motorcycle was no different.

So Shane is showing off, flying around the block like Evil Knievel, until all of a sudden we look down the driveway and here comes Vince with that big barreled chest and he's huffing and puffing as he charges right toward us.

"Boys, where's Shane?" None of us were going to rat out our boy, but then again, none of us had to because a couple of seconds later the knucklehead comes flying around the corner on the motorcycle. Vince just looks at us and says, "Boys, time to go home," and we all jumped in the car. But as we started the engine, we could see Vince grab Shane and use his head like a battering ram to open the front door. We started laughing because we knew Shane was going to catch hell for what he did, but that's just the way we all were . . . we all just laughed at each other's pain, and Shane felt some serious pain for riding that motorcycle, believe me.

Like I said, it was never boring hanging out with Shane. Our lives back then always involved a lot of alcohol and a lot of action. And, usually, it was about trying to hurt each other in front of everyone else just to get a laugh. We'd shoot each other with BB guns, drive in Shane's Corvette convertible through the snow with the top down, just whatever dumb thing we could think of doing.

And that's where the idea of the Mean Street Posse came from. We were a crew long before we were on TV. The only difference was, in real life, Shane was the only one with any money. And that's really the biggest misconception people have when it came to our characters. Since we were real-life friends with Shane, everyone assumed we were all rich. But that's just not true at all. Rodney's father owns the family upholstery business, and they're very blue collar. By no means do they live a lavish lifestyle. My father was a police officer for a bunch of years, then ended up being a plumber for the last twenty years of his life. He was one of those guys who would drive over two hours from Greenwich to New London, Connecticut, just to make a few extra bucks and did whatever he could to make ends meet. Back in the day, he bought our house in Greenwich for $30,000. To him, his mortgage was $100 a month, and the house he really wanted was $35,000, but he was afraid the payment was too high. That house today is worth $2 million and my mom's house is probably close to $1 million, but back then, we were living paycheck to paycheck.

In fact, I didn't even get my first car until the day my dad died, taking over his pickup truck. So unlike what people thought of us and the "mean streets" of Greenwich, it's not like we were all riding around in our own Beamers or Benzes. We never went on family vacations. We just didn't have that kind of money. So that's why when you see the characters on TV and the crazy stunts, that was us, we really lived that (sometimes) dangerous aspect of the Posse . . . but the money, that was all Shane.

* * *

Behind the scenes, Chris Chambers from WWE TV came up with the idea for the Mean Street Posse along with Vince Russo and Ed Ferrara, and the original idea was based from the movie *The Outsiders*. You had the Greasers and Socs, and the Socs were the rich kids that everyone hated. We took those characters and added our own flavor. This was back in 1999, and Shane was working toward a match at WrestleMania against X-Pac. They were looking for ways to bring real heat on Shane's character— they really wanted the crowd to hate him—so they made him this badass from Greenwich, Connecticut, and brought us in to help, but we were only supposed to be there for a couple of weeks.

A couple of weeks that turned into the best three years of my life.

Chapter 2

The Deal

Back in 1999, I was really struggling to find my way in life. I'd go to work, work out at the gym, hit the bars … rinse and repeat. I wanted more out of life, but I just didn't know what or how. That all changed thanks to Shane.

Shane had not only joined the family business but was a regular on *Raw*, WWE's flagship television program. And I'll never forget it. Shane called me and Rodney into his office one Friday and said he needed a favor. I figured he needed help with something around the house or was trying to plan a big weekend out or something. Back then, Shane used to give us security key cards to the WWE building so we could work out in their gym for free, so we were already at Titan Tower when we asked to speak with us. So after an hour of hitting the weights we head up to his office. That's when Shane looks at us with a smirk and asks: "What are you guys doing Sunday morning?" We had nothing going on, so he says that he wants us to dress really preppy. He holds up this script that the writers wrote for us. He wants us to make our WWE debut as the Mean Street Posse on *Raw*. Rodney and I were laughing hysterically, thinking he was pulling a prank and bullshitting us, but Shane was dead serious. He wanted us to be on *Raw*. We couldn't stop laughing, but Shane is holding this script and he's showing us what they want us to say, and then he rips the thing to shreds. *Holy shit, did we just blow our chance to actually be on* Raw? But then Shane said: "Fuck these stories. I want you to go in there and tell stories about when we were kids, running from the cops and getting into fights. I want the stories as believable as possible. Chris Chambers is going to film these stories, cut them up, and we're going to show them on *Monday Night Raw* the following night."

Rodney and I were thrilled. I don't think either one of us caught a wink of sleep that night. I know I had all these stories I wanted to tell running through my head, but at the same time, the WWE is one of those things where you might get a shot to make it but you won't get a second shot if you blow it, so I was fucking nervous as hell. Sunday morning rolled around quicker than I could've ever anticipated, and with no sleep and a stomach doing back flips, I knew we had to shine. Rodney and I were supposed to head to the studio around 10 a.m., but Rodney came over to my house at 8 a.m. with a plan that included about twenty-four beers, as we needed something to take the edge off or we were never going to be able to face the cameras.

We cracked our first beer at a quarter after eight. We both had close to a 12-pack before we arrived at the studio, and ended up doing all these interviews about what it was like on the "mean streets" of Greenwich. Watch them back on the WWE Network today and you can see my face is red, as I was feeling a pretty good buzz, but I was so nervous I figured that was the only way I'd make it through, and I knew I had to deliver.

Anyway, they filmed the various vignettes, and then comes Monday night and we're on TV. I remember when we first showed up at the Pepsi Arena. This was our first live event, and it was at Albany, New York. We had to be there at 11 a.m., and there were crowds and crowds of people waiting outside the wrestler's parking lot when we pulled up, just hanging out and waiting to get autographs. I couldn't believe how much passion the fans had and how much they really wanted to meet the wrestlers. They would call out your name and hold up signs and whistle, anything to try and get your attention. We walked through the door and there were boxes everywhere and handwritten signs on the wall that said men's locker room with an arrow one way, and women's locker room with an arrow pointed in the opposite direction. Then as you walked toward the locker room you saw the gorilla position. Named after Gorilla Monsoon, it is where Vince or whoever is running the show that night sits, and there is a TV screen and a microphone so they can communicate with the announcers and the referees. I remember walking through and trying not to mark out like a fan, but I was and still am a huge WWE fan, so in my head I'm walking by all these guys and I'm like, *Oh my god, there's Edge, there's the Rock, there's Road Dogg.* These were guys who I loved to watch and now I wasn't just walking by them backstage, but now I was on the same show! What was I even doing there? And I could feel that they were looking at us with the same question in mind. And I could tell that they didn't really like us being there. Nobody at that point knew we were going to be there more than just a couple of weeks, and I think they were frustrated that our vignettes had been getting so much air time on *Raw*. We finally get to the locker room and meet Blue Meanie and Stevie Richards, who were two lower card guys, were cool from the start and a lot more accepting of us than the bigger stars. And while some people would talk to us, a lot of the other wrestlers seemed very hesitant, like they didn't know what to make of us. It's like meeting anyone for the first time: you're not going to open up and tell them your life story, so we could tell that it was out of politeness that most people even talked to us at all.

The next thing we knew, with our heads still spinning, Shane comes up to us in the locker room. We had no idea what we were even there to do, so he puts his arm around us and leads us out to the ring. A bunch of the Attitude Era's biggest stars were going over their matches and talking about what they were going to do. We sat there and watched guys work out and decide on move sequences they wanted to pull off later that night. It was amazing to see up close like this. It's a fan's dream come true, but here we were, not just fans, but were actually going to be part of the act. Eventually it came to the point where we met with Jack Lanza, who was one of the agents for the show. His job was to go over in detail our roles for the night and how we were to go about helping Shane by jumping X-Pac. Then we all walked outside to the parking lot where they showed us the Corvette convertible we were going to drive up in. I'm trying to soak this all in and everything is going great—until we start hearing loud bangs all around us. Something was hitting against the metal garage door we were standing next to. We couldn't figure out what was happening, but the noises were getting louder and louder, and when we looked up, we could see that across the street, there was this four-story parking garage and fans had made it to the top floor. There were guys who obviously didn't like the Mean Street Posse and were hocking quarters at us. They missed, thank god, but the sound of these quarters banging against the garage door was echoing throughout the parking lot. Jack Lanza ran and got security to chase the guys away, but we knew right then that *nobody* liked the Mean Street Posse. This was our first live event and we were already under attack. We had some serious heat because of our vignettes, and everything just kept snowballing from there. Must have been the sweaters.

* * *

So the night finally came, and what's crazy is our debut actually occurred on a pretty historic night of wrestling. It was the same night (March 22, 1999) Stone Cold drove the Coors Light truck into the arena, pulled out a hose from the truck, and sprayed Vince, Shane, and the Rock with beer. Shane had challenged X-Pac to a street fight outside the arena and as he and Shane started going at it, two Corvette convertibles pull up, and at that time, there were five of us in the Mean Street Posse, and we all jump out, grab X-Pac, and then we held him while Shane beat up on him. Once X-Pac was down, we hauled ass out of there in the Corvettes. Luckily, no more quarters were flying at us from across the street.

We did our job, and the crowd hated us for it. But the thing about the wrestling business, and especially working for the McMahons, is you just never know where you stand or what will happen next. You're always in the dark until the very last second.

Even when we weren't wrestling, I'd ask Shane what was going to happen on *Raw* and all he'd say is: "You'll have to watch." But we never knew what *we* were going to do, how *we'd* be involved, or where the story was going the entire time *we* were in WWE. Nobody would tell us anything. We would just show up at the arena and find out on the spot. Same thing goes for Wrestle-Mania. The week after *Raw*, we were told to go to Mania, so I rented a Ford Explorer, piled all the guys in, including original Posse members (Rodney, Willie Green, Billy Piro, and Chris Szczechowicz), packed a cooler full of beer, and drove down to Philly for the show.

For the first time we were part of the entire WrestleMania weekend, and people were actually asking *us* for autographs . . . it was crazy! Walking around the locker room, I felt like *I* should be the one asking for signatures, but now there were fans out there that wanted a picture or an autograph from the Mean Street Posse.

But the biggest thrill at the time was that we were not only going to WrestleMania but were asked to get involved in Shane's match. So there we are, sitting in the front row, and behind us were several players from the New York Giants. Now I'm a huge football fan, so I'm pointing them out like, there's this star or that star; meanwhile, they start pointing at me. They were like, "There's Pete Gas! There's Rodney!" It was cool as hell. Isaac Hayes was sitting two seats away from us—there were stars all around—and they were just as interested in us as we were in them. I remember looking up in the crowd in between matches, seeing all the signs people had, and I'm like, "Rodney, look at that!" There were about ten signs with our names on it. Mean Street Posse signs, Pete Gas signs, Rodney signs . . . I couldn't believe it. And the good thing about it was, the WWE has people backstage who look out for that stuff, so we were on our way.

They say that once you have signs, you're over with the crowd in some way. Whether they love you or hate you, they care enough to get a piece of oak tag and take the time to make a sign about you. That means you're connecting with the people in a big way, and that really means something. So to be completely honest, I really owe it to all of the fans who brought signs to WrestleMania, because the office saw them, and what was supposed to be a few weeks' run with Shane ended up turning into something a lot bigger.

But I'll never forget that WrestleMania. During Shane's match with X-Pac, the plan was for Shane to send X-Pac toward us, and then we were supposed to hold him while Shane beat him up. X-Pac broke out of my grasp and hit me with an elbow. That part was all planned. But what I decided to do was jump back and take a back bump onto my chair after he hit me with the elbow. So I take the bump and go flying back, and I start holding my chest like X-Pac has the sharpest elbows in the world; like he hit me with Wolverine's claws or something. I'm lying there and I knew the cameras were on me, so I'm selling it like I'm really hurt. It was just my natural reaction from watching wrestling for all those years. I wanted to put X-Pac over the best I could, and the fact that I sold this injury—and the fact that Rodney really sold his injury as well—helped trigger something in the office that the Mean Street Posse needed to stick around . . . we just didn't know it yet.

* * *

We headed home after WrestleMania, back to our normal 9-to-5 lives.

Then about ten days later, here comes Shane again, and he wants to see us back in his office. The first thing he did when we walked in was hand us both envelopes. "What the hell is this?" I asked. All he said was, "Thank you," and when we looked in the envelopes there were checks inside. Nothing was ever mentioned about money, and I actually thought we were just doing it as a favor to Shane. But now we were getting paid a few thousand dollars each out of nowhere. We would've done it for free, but who's complaining? Next thing he asked was, "How much vacation time do you have left with your jobs?" Back then, *Monday Night Raw* was filmed every other week. So they would hold *Raw* live on Monday, and then tape the following week's episode on Tuesday. There was no *SmackDown* at the time, so when there was a pay-per-view, you would wrestle Sunday, Monday, Tuesday, but would then be off for two weeks. All of the regular guys would still be doing house shows across the country, but since we were only doing television, that was our schedule, and Shane wanted us to continue running this way for a few months more (or so he told us).

I was currently running the office for a production company called Lightnin' Rentals. Essentially, I rented movie equipment to production companies and worked with shows like *The Sopranos* and *Oz*, and movies like *The Thomas Crown Affair*. So I was on movie sets working, but I was a one-man crew, meeting with the directors and the transportation captains in the movie industry while at the same time prepping and cleaning trucks, and making sure the portable toilets are emptied and all the fluids have been refilled so they can move on to the next shoot. So when I was out wrestling, it put a strain on the relationship with my bosses because I was taking three or four days off every two weeks. They were happy for me, but at the same time they had their own business to run, though we tried to work together and balance it as best we could. I couldn't quit my full-time job because I didn't know how long this wrestling gig would last. All I knew was that the longer I was on TV and in the ring, the more I got addicted to being a WWE Superstar.

Chapter 3

Corporate Posse

We sat in the front row with Shane at WrestleMania, then ten days later were on the road with the rest of the crew. Then, on April 12 in Detroit, Michigan, we were about to make our way to the ring with no training other than what we knew from being a wrestling fan and watching *Raw* every Monday. The whole "Corporation" was down in the squared-circle: the Rock, Big Bossman, Shane, Test, Ken Shamrock, Triple H, Chyna, Gerald Brisco, and Pat Patterson. What happened was, Shane ended up introducing the two newest members of the Corporation, and it was Rodney and me, and we were greeted with this overwhelming chorus of boos. We had heat instantly because they hated Shane so much, but at the same time we still saw a few sweater vests in the crowd, so we knew that even with the crowd jeering us we were making some kind of connection, and that's always a good thing. The storyline had Shane and Vince fighting for control of the company, with Shane eventually slapping Vince in the face, telling him he wasn't his father anymore, and then firing Vince's longtime friends Brisco and Patterson (a.k.a. the Stooges). My facial expression on the show says it all, as Shane didn't hold back on that slap. I think he was getting him back for that motorcycle incident in front of his house. Then again, it's one of the things they teach you early on in this business: sometimes you need to really lay it in to get your point across. And boy, did Shane ever get his point across that night.

A couple of segments later, Shane is pissed off at Mick Foley, and since Foley spent a lot of time hanging out in boiler rooms back then, the Posse was ordered to enter the boiler room and beat him up. *Raw* came back from a commercial, and we were getting our asses kicked by Mick. Rodney was already partially laid out and I was literally thrown out the boiler room door.

Achievement Unlocked:
I got my first official ass kicking on *Raw* by none other than the legend himself, Mick Foley. Not a bad night's work.

Working with Mick was always great. He understood how green we were, especially in the beginning, and always worked with us in order for us to better understand what to do and why we were doing it. This was a tremendous help because we were thrown right into the fire—from funny vignettes to getting our ass kicked by one of the all-time greats in a boiler room. I think

Vince and Shane worked it out so that we worked against the people who would help us the most and not just try to bury us because we were friends of the family. The boiler room was also memorable for me because that's when we came up with the slogan, "Every single day, somebody's got to pay!" It was our first catch phrase, and the funny thing is that it's a shady slogan one of my old bosses used to say when I worked at this used car lot. People would come in with bad credit and he'd sell them a car at a super high interest rate. Then when he walked in the office, he'd tell us, "Every single day, somebody's got to pay." I just thought that phrase fit so well with our slimy Greenwich characters. I never would've guessed that some crappy job I had years prior would come back and pay dividends (let alone that one).

The following week, we were called down to the announcer's table to do commentary for the Mick Foley vs. Triple H match. I remember the microphones were really bad and it was hard to hear what we were all saying, but again, it was trial by fire. I had never done anything like this before, and here we were on *Raw* attempting to do commentary with bad mics. Luckily this was one of the shows taped on Tuesday, so we were able to go into the studio and re-do our commentary while watching the show back on TV. When we did the commentary the first time, we thought everything we were saying was going into the show, and that's a lot of pressure. And it's a whole different experience being down at the announcer's table than just watching it on TV in the back or from home. To me, attempting to do commentary from the table was harder than going into the ring for the first time. There's no script, everything's ad-libbed, and when you have zero experience and are told to go out there and talk about these characters and the storyline, it's a lot harder than you'd think. You try to be funny, you want to be entertaining, but if you ham it up too much then you come off as annoying and you might never get that opportunity again. So I just tried to be myself, and when I heard it back, I didn't think it turned out as bad as I thought it would. But then we get called back to the studio and we find out we have to do it again, but by then at least we knew what to expect from ourselves and from the match, so we were able to work it out a little bit better on the second take. The main thing is, you don't want to talk over Jim Ross and Jerry "The King" Lawler, but then when you think about it, you're there to take over the conversation. That's what heels do. Let them control the play-by-play, but then you have to speak your piece and say what you're out there to say. You're out there for a reason: to help sell the story. And if you don't speak, you're useless. It's a fine line to walk. I thought we'd get some advice from King or J. R. heading into the match, but neither one really said much. Thankfully King hit us with questions during the match to feed us right into the storyline, which helped keep the conversation flowing. We were always kept in the dark, and then to find out that we were going to be working at the announcer's table, that was definitely a shock. We weren't really able to take too many bumps back then, so they figured the more we talked, the more we would be able to establish our characters as heels without having to actually get inside the ring.

That same night, we had one of our first face-to-face encounters with an angry fan. We're in Grand Rapids, Michigan, and it's the night Stone Cold drives his monster truck over Rock's town car. That night, we had parked our car in a spot really close to where the fans had access. So we go to leave the arena and I volunteered to get the car so Rodney and Shane didn't have to go outside. We were so hated at this point that they didn't want to deal with people throwing shit at us. I tell them that I'll put our stuff in the trunk and then they can run out and we'll leave before anyone sees us. So I go out there and the crowd starts chanting "Mean Street Pussies!" and there is one guy who is right by the trunk of our car, and he had to be 6-foot-6, 300 pounds.

This guy was all over me, calling me every name he could think of, telling me I suck, but I wouldn't turn around. I didn't want to act like it bothered me. But then I decided for whatever reason that I wanted to see what he'd do if I walked toward him. So I put everything in the trunk and walked right up to him and looked him in the eyes and was like, "Hey, how are you doing?" And the guy was stunned. All he could say was, "Good." I ask him, "How did you like the show tonight?" And he says, "Stone Cold is the man!" So I say to him, "What do you think of the Mean Street Posse?" And he goes, "I think you guys suck! I'd like to kick your ass!" I tell him, "That's good, that means I'm doing what I'm supposed to be doing. I'm supposed to be playing a rich kid who is here to piss you off, so if that's what I'm doing and that's how you feel, thanks for the compliment."

You ever see the reaction of a dog when they give you the head tilt? That was the look on this guy's face as he tried to register what just happened. All of a sudden, this guy becomes my buddy, and from the time the Mean Street Posse left that parking lot, he had a fist pump going as he chanted "Pete Gas! Pete Gas! Pete Gas!" He was my number one fan. Shane used to tell us all the time, if they believe it's real, let them believe it's real and let them have fun with it. I remember the time Stephanie slapped her mom and people would come up to us and ask, "How could Shane let Stephanie slap her mom like that?" If they have to believe that the McMahons are fighting, then I'd reply with, "Well, Shane doesn't like to talk about the problems his family is going through right now." You just go along with it and it's funny to see the reaction out of people who still believe it's real. But then when you go out of your way and talk to fans, then most are like this big guy who wanted to kick my ass at first ... but by the end of the night, they're chanting your name.

The only bad part of this story is, that was the last night WWE let Shane ride from town to town with the Posse. Word came down from Vince that we had to separate. Vince felt that if we didn't, then we'd never earn the respect from the boys. Vince didn't want it to appear that there was any favoritism going on in the locker room or behind the scenes. Besides, the three of us together spelled trouble since day one, but it's not like we were taking out picket fences like the old days. So while I wish we could've continued to ride together, in the long run it made total sense.

The following week was April 26, and we showed up for *Raw* on the night after Backlash. During the pay-per-view, Stephanie was abducted by the Undertaker and nobody knew where she was. Shane had been the special guest referee in the Stone Cold vs. Rock match, which led to beef between Shane and Rock, which set up a match the following night on *Raw* in Hartford, Connecticut.

So the match begins between Shane and Rock and thirty seconds later we run into the ring and Rock kicks our asses. That's the night I received my first Rock Bottom.

Before Rock could give Shane the People's Elbow, Triple H came in and started beating on the Rock, followed shortly by Chyna. When the referees came down to break up the fight, Rodney, Shane, and I each grabbed a referee while Triple H and Chyna continued their beat down.

Later that night is when Undertaker brought Stephanie out on that Taker Cross and tried to marry her before Stone Cold finally ran down and saved the day. It's funny to look back on these nights because so much was happening and there were so many great storylines interwoven throughout each episode. That night, *Raw* went off the air with Vince thanking Stone Cold, only thing is, nobody knew at the time that Vince was actually the Higher Power all along.

At the time, in real life, Stephanie and Triple H weren't even a couple yet. They didn't start dating until September 1999; it wasn't until their storylines started to mix together that they fell in love. When they were playing husband and wife on TV, they would flirt with each other, and it got to the point where Triple H asked her out for real, but they kept it a secret from the locker room because they didn't want to create any drama behind the scenes with Triple H dating the boss's daughter.

> Unfortunately, that also meant the end of Triple H and Chyna, both on screen and off. I really want to add how much I respected Chyna, especially since she was such a big part of the Attitude Era, and I think she gets lost in the discussion when people look back on that period in the organization's history. Not only was she a phenomenal worker, she really was one of the sweetest people in the locker room. She went through a hard time breaking into the business, as a lot of the guys didn't accept her because of the way she looked. She wasn't gorgeous like some of the other divas back then, not to mention, she was bigger and stronger than some of the guys on the roster. And, because of that, some people weren't very nice to her and I think that took its toll. When she was dating Triple H, she had this confidence about her that you just

didn't see before. She also had various rounds of plastic surgery, so she became more and more feminine-looking and attractive as time went on. Then, because of her size and her ability in the ring, that enabled the writers to do some great things with her character, including winning the Intercontinental Championship and entering the Royal Rumble.

But as a person, she was always really, really sweet. One time we were in the gym and she wanted to know if I wanted to do a leg workout with her. She and I and Chaz from the Headbangers were doing leg presses and the set was that you had to do 10 reps of about 90-percent of your max weight, then you got to take 10 seconds of rest. Then nine reps with nine seconds or rest and so on, until you had to instantly work your way right back up to 10. It was a shock to the system. It was an unbelievable workout, but was brutal to the point where it gave you wobbly legs. She kicked our asses and made it looks so easy. Her work ethic was just phenomenal. She was a student of the business, trained by Killer Kowalski and, as great as she was in the ring, she was an even greater friend. No one ever had a bad thing to say about her. If you had a problem, you could always go to her directly. Hearing of her passing really hurt. She was such a good person, but she fell on hard times. It's one of the heartbreaking things about the industry. So many people die young. She used to tell us about all the hard times she had breaking in, but by the time we got there she was already a star, and so many fans would go crazy for her because she had everything from the look to the ability. It must've been a really hard ride to go from having no friends to being one of the most popular characters on the roster in a matter of years. The fans were cheering so loud for her, but you learn that those people yelling aren't your friends, and no matter how many people chant your name, if you don't have that support outside the ring, this business can be brutal.

Chapter 4

Learning the Ropes

As someone who grew up a wrestling fan, I have to say how crazy even the littlest things were for me to see backstage. Even just wandering around and seeing the locker room blew my mind. The size of the locker room always depends on the venue. If there are a lot of locker rooms, sometimes you'll get the mid-card guys in one area and the main event guys in a different section. I always liked the arenas that had just one big locker room, that way we were all in the same space. Even so, there wasn't too much trouble in terms of egos during the Attitude Era. I had heard years prior that Macho Man had to have his own locker room so Miss Elizabeth could change, and Hulk had to have his own, and Warrior had to have his own. When I was there, if the arena had one big locker room, everyone shared and nobody was harping on about not having their own space. If you walked through, you'd see Big Show's gear hanging in one area with Mark Henry's gear hanging in the next locker over. Everyone would be out at catering having lunch, but it was amazing to get to walk through the backstage area and see everyone's gear out like that. It was definitely a cool atmosphere. And it's funny, because I always dreamed of being a wrestler and now, because of my relationship with Shane, not only was I on *Raw* but the Mean Street Posse was actually making a name for ourselves.

It's insane to look back on, though, because way before any of this happened, I asked Shane for a shot to join WWE back in 1992, and he straight up shot me down. When Shane joined the family business, Vince had him learn all facets. He spent time working in every department (big and small) to get the feel for the business because, back then, he was the heir apparent of the company. He was trying to establish himself, and I remember he eventually had his own office, his own assistant.

When I went to see him about becoming a wrestler for the first time, I was at a crossroads in life. I had always wanted to be a wrestler, but now I had a job. I figured, if I didn't go for it then, and this was back in 1992 (seven years before the Posse's debut), that I was never going to do it. So I approached Shane for my shot at pursuing my dream. I used to just go to Shane's office all the time and we'd bust each other's balls, but this time I went in with a purpose. I said to him, "Hey Shane, what do I have to do to be involved in the business?" He was downplaying it, telling me I didn't want to get involved. He told me: "You have to pay your dues. You have to train in Memphis, Tennessee, and work for $25 a night. You have to work from the bottom, setting up the ring, and you're treated like shit. You end up losing every match and they beat the hell out of you in the ring. And before that, you have to go to wrestling school, and you have to hope that it's a reputable school and not just some guy taking your money." If I wanted to pursue it at that point, he would've pointed me in the right direction, but he was trying to make it look as unappealing as possible. He knew the industry was tough, and knew I already had a job and was established. Plus, being educated, I had the opportunity to make money without putting my body on the line. And I'm sure part of it is that he didn't want to turn down a friend if it came down to that time and I didn't have it. Maybe he didn't want to be the one to say, hey, you suck. What's ironic is, he kept talking about how I'd have to train in Memphis, Tennessee, and I'd have to work the Mid-South region piling into cars while working through your bank account because you can't really hold down a job during training. You need to get to the venue by 3 p.m. just to set up the ring at some high school gym or armory, then you do your match later in the night, and when the show is over you need to tear down the ring and drive back. By this time, it's like 10 p.m. What are you going to do, work the graveyard shift at McDonalds? No job will allow you the flexibility to hold down a wrestling career at the same time. During the week, you're constantly training, so there's no time for full-time employment. It tells you a lot about the guys who sacrifice so much in order to "pay their dues." When you're working for $25 a night, you're basically eating potatoes to survive. You have to tip your hat to guys like Stone Cold Steve Austin who worked so hard, ate potatoes for so long, before finally becoming the biggest draw in the entire industry. He made it, but for every Austin, there are thousands of guys who lose their dream somewhere along the way.

For the Mean Street Posse, we just happened to get a break. We were brought in to play our role as Shane's friends, and we could feel the resentment behind the scenes. I mean you can't blame them, as we didn't pay the same dues of everyone else in the locker room. We hadn't even gone to wrestling school. Had no training whatsoever, and we were being featured on *Raw*, so we understood the way they felt. Hell, I'd probably feel the same exact way.

In the beginning, nobody thought we'd be around longer than a couple of weeks. Everyone figured we were just a quirky act to help promote WrestleMania and then we'd be gone, so they were pleasant and joked around with us, but that was mainly because we were Shane's friends. Shane was incredibly well liked backstage with the boys. When he was a part of the ring crew while paying his own dues, he traveled on the road with the Nasty Boys, so he was accepted as not just the boss's son, but as one of their friends. So everyone was getting a kick out of us at first, but when we came back after WrestleMania, the joking kind of stopped. They must have all been looking at us, wondering, "Why are these guys still here?" They were still friendly to us, but people were jealous of the amount of air time we were getting and the storylines we were involved in. Nobody ignored us and everyone was friendly, but sometimes I felt like the friendliness was forced, like they didn't want us to be around. I think some people looked down at us because of our relationship with Shane. But what's funny is, some of the people who weren't the warmest when we started ended up being the ones who, as time went on, became some of my closest friends. Take Test, for example. He didn't really have much to say to us at the beginning, but one of his friends, Prince Albert, was great to us. Then again, we knew Prince Albert prior to joining the roster, because he used to work out at Titan Tower while trying out for the WWE so we'd see him and Val Venis there when we'd go to the gym. They had seen us around before and so accepted us right away.

But Vince's thing is, he gives the fans what they want, no matter who you know or how many friends you have in the back. Whether it was the Mean Street Posse or whoever, if you're getting a reaction from the crowd, Vince sees that, hears that, and does his best to capitalize on the situation. The saying goes, do what's best for business. And that's what Vince does. We were playing the roles of two snotty rich kids from Greenwich, and people love to hate that stuff. It's like with Stone Cold. They all want to give their boss the finger. They all want the ability to pour a beer over their boss's head or kick their ass and get away with it. Same with hating the rich kids who have it all. It's an easy sell to boo the guys in the sweaters and Corvettes.

But I have to say, while some guys resented our new spot, it was the superstars like Stone Cold and Triple H who went out of their way to try and help us. About a month into the business, there was a house show (not televised) at Madison Square Garden featuring Stone Cold vs. the Rock. We were in the Rock's corner because we were in the Corporation at the time. During the match, Rock was starting to get the best of Austin and he goes to shoot Stone Cold into the ropes where Rodney and I are on the apron, and we're going to hit him. But Stone Cold reverses it, and, of course, we end up hitting the Rock. Then Rock gets a Stone Cold Stunner and the 1-2-3. Rock rolls out of the ring afterward and Stone Cold is in the ring celebrating his win with a few Steveweisers. We go up to the Rock and we're like, "We're sorry, we screwed up, how can we make this up to you?" He says, "You want to make it up to 'The Rock?' Get him!" So I go running at Stone Cold with the Polish Hammer, but he kicks me in the gut and gives me a Stunner, then hits Rodney with the same thing and leaves us lying in the middle of the ring. He then goes and gets a couple more beers, clicks them together, and pours them all over us. We're lying there like we're knocked out, and after Stone Cold does his thing, he leaves the ring, and then Rock slides back in. The Rock looks at both of us and ends up giving us the double People's Elbow and the crowd goes crazy.

That was the good part.

The bad part? We didn't know how to take the Stunner well and I guess we didn't take it the way Stone Cold wanted us to. We had never done it before, and I think that made Austin a little nervous about working with us in the future. The biggest thing that bothered him, though, was the way we performed the move, especially since the match was at the Garden. I remember him being backstage and explaining to us how to take the Stunner afterward. "You have to understand, this is Madison Square Garden, and the thing about Madison Square Garden is, this is where wrestling was born." To most wrestlers, performing at MSG is like the Holy Grail, so whenever you see a match there you'll notice the punches are a little harder and the kicks are a little stiffer because everyone is trying to look their best on the main stage (even for a house show). The intensity level of every match is just so much higher any time you're performing there, and he was worried his Stunner came off bad because of how we took it. Even though it wasn't televised, it was something he was concerned about.

Two days later, we had the privilege of working with Stone Cold and Triple H in the ring again, only this time it was prior to the doors opening and we were just working on the basics.

I remember Triple H was trying to find some moves that we could do so we could work a few matches. He was trying to show us how he throws a punch and how he snaps the heel of his front foot on the mat. I'm still amazed how, with his toes on the ground, how loud his heel hits the mat when he throws a punch. You can hear it in the back row of an arena—that's how much snap he gets. Stone Cold then took over and was working with us more on how to take the Stunner. A couple of weeks later, Shane was working against Stone Cold in Anaheim in a steel cage match back in May 1999. Again, this was another house show and after Shane loses, I run into the ring and get hit with the Stunner. Rodney then gets Stunned, and Stone Cold throws us both through the door so we're sprawled out on the steps outside the ring. Austin proceeds to climb up the cage and pours beer on us from the top and the crowd goes wild.

Meanwhile, Shane is in the ring, and Stone Cold gives him a beer, but when Shane drinks it, Austin gives him the Stunner and Shane spits beer everywhere as he takes the move. After this goes on for a while, Stone Cold finally leaves and we enter the ring to help Shane. I remember, we each put an arm of Shane's around us as we walked down the aisle toward backstage. The aisle was only about 6-feet wide, so we didn't have much room, and while we're trying to maneuver a fan reached over and punched me in the side of the head. He hit me pretty good. I mean, this guy hit me like he believed this shit was real. I immediately jumped out of character and wanted to kill this guy, but security got to him first and dragged his ass to the back. I went back there and really wanted a piece of the guy, but was told to just mind my own business and security would take care of it.

Chapter 5

How a Match Works

When we first started in the ring, we really had no clue what we were doing. What we made sure to do was try and soak in as much as the veterans were teaching us about the business and how a match actually worked as possible. It's well known that the Undertaker is the master of matches. He told me one time how he lets the crowd dictate how the match will go. Sure, you know the ending and a few big spots you're going to hit, but beyond that you're working to the crowd. A match is supposed to be like an emotional roller coaster. There are moves to get the crowd up and down, up and down, then the end is like an orgasm. If the heel wins, you get the crowd pissed off, or you have the baby-face come back and win, which sends the crowd into a frenzy. Whatever the case, you're making every move with the crowd involved. I remember when Kurt Angle was just starting out, he was going to have a match against the Undertaker and wanted to go over the match before it started, but all Taker said was: "I'll see you out there, kid." Taker wanted to put Angle through a test, and Angle was so nervous, but when he came back, he couldn't believe what he had just experienced. He said how Taker was talking to him the entire time in the ring, calling the spots, and Angle learned a lesson through that experience of how to work a crowd. Just by watching matches like that, everyone in the locker room is able to learn through Undertaker on how to call matches. Later in my training, I was sent to Puerto Rico, were I was trained by Savio Vega. I learned that if you got shot into the ropes and I showed you my elbow, you knew I would hit you with the elbow. That was your cue, here it comes. Or if I shoot you in and say, "Duck two, elbow," that means I'm going to shoot you into the ropes, you're going to duck my first move, hit the ropes, duck my second move, hit the ropes again, then I'm going to hit you with the elbow. You learn, and the best way to learn is to be out there and doing it.

Words cannot express how great it is to hit moves like that on the fly and have it come off looking great. It's one of the best feelings you can have in this business. The referee also plays a large role in the match. A few hours before *Raw*, a card is posted around the arena with all of the matches. It will say something like, Pete Gas vs. Val Venis, Pat Patterson is the agent. We will then go see the agent, and Pat Patterson has been in a production meeting since 11 a.m. going over the entire show and has been fine-tuning this script since Thursday morning's writers' meeting. So now, Pat Patterson will say, "Val, you're going over tonight. Pete, you're going to slip out at one point to get a chair. The referee is going to grab the chair from you and argue, and from there, Val is going to hit you, set up his finisher, and go over with the 1-2-3."

Here is how the roller coaster works. The crowd hates me because I'm being a real son of a bitch by grabbing a chair, but then they start to come around once the referee gets in my way. By the time Val hits me with his finisher, they're going through the roof when the music hits. So when we'd see Pat, he'd give us the finish, then tell us, "You have eight minutes to do this match." So then Val and I would get together and work out our signature moves. But that eight minutes starts the second the first wrestler's music hits for his entrance. So now you're working backwards on the match. If you figure the ending is going to take one minute and fifteen seconds, you really book yourself one minute and thirty seconds because:

A) You're on live television;

B) You want to give the announcers time to talk about the match and show the replay;

C) If you go over, Vince will go to commercial and be so pissed that your ass won't be on TV the following week.

So you want to give that ending some extra time. So now we went from eight minutes, you take away 90 seconds, and now we're down to six and a half minutes. You figure both of our entrances take 30 seconds and you're down to just over five minutes for the rest of the match. And that's if you're lucky, because I can't tell you how many times you're told that you will get eight minutes, but then right before the match starts your time is cut to four minutes because the segment before you went too long. Rock's promos used to always go longer than the time he was allotted, so the entire schedule would change on the fly. So if Rock's being long winded, then we have half our time, and you go with a shorter version of a finish and hope it all works out. You'll notice during matches how every referee has an earpiece. Well there's a guy sitting in the back with a stopwatch and a microphone, and he tells the referee when it's time to wrap things up. The referee will then whisper to the wrestlers to bring it home, and you then move right to whatever ending you already have in place. There are so many moving pieces, it's amazing to witness behind the scenes. The average fan has no idea.

And that's just the kind of stuff we were learning as we tried to catch up physically to the spot we were given on *Raw*. When we weren't on TV, we were back to our full-time jobs, then would head over to the WWE corporate office at night to work with Dr. Tom Pritchard, who became our wrestling instructor. We'd get back from the road on Wednesday and, depending on how bad we got our asses kicked on Monday and Tuesday, Dr. Tom might give us Wednesday to recover. If not, we were back in the ring practicing that same night after working 9-5. Sometimes, depending on our work schedule, we were back in the gym Wednesday afternoon. We'd be so tired that we'd call in sick to our actual jobs on Thursday or Friday, but then Dr. Tom would call us into the gym for practice, so we'd be there. We were constantly grinding, trying to make ourselves better for the next time we'd be on *Raw*. And we weren't even under contract at this time! Just think if we would've been really injured practicing or at *Raw*. It's crazy to think about it now, but not being under contract, we were taking some huge risks. It was never really discussed, but we went out there and threw our bodies around because that's what we wanted to do. We hoped it would all pay off, so we were willing to put in the hard work and take that chance.

But I loved being in the ring and wrestling in front of a live crowd. I don't think there was ever a time we ran out there where I didn't have a healthy case of nerves, and that's a good thing. It keeps you on edge. No matter what I did, I tried to run things through my head and, to me, having those nerves made me focus on what I had to do in order to get everything right and not hurt anyone, including myself.

I remember the first time going out in front of a live audience and having to run down that ramp. You practice walking down during rehearsal, and it might sound stupid, but all I could think about was, "Don't trip, don't trip." I was so afraid I was going to fall down and make an ass out of myself, we'd never get invited back. It's funny now, because when I look back at it, if I did trip, it might have been even funnier because our characters were already screw-ups. It wouldn't have been Shockmaster bad. It really would have fit in with what the Mean Street Posse was all about.

I remember seeing someone trip one time when they were getting in the ring because their foot got caught between the second and third rope, so once I didn't trip on the ramp, I just wanted to make sure my foot didn't get caught in the rope. At first I was careful with every step, but after a while it all becomes second nature.

The other thing you don't realize as a fan has to do with the ropes and just how hard they are to run against. When you first get into the ring and grab that rope, you think, "It's a rope, how do you get any spring?" But then you hit the rope and you realize that it's pretty hard. Watch *Tough Enough* and you'll see that these wrestlers will have bruises on the side of their back and under their armpits. I remember when I got that same thing. You keep hitting that same area and your skin begins to callus. After a while, it doesn't bruise anymore, but it's tough to get used to at first. But that's not the only misleading part of the ring: the ring itself is built from a steel frame that features steel poles and steel rods. There's a very thin layer of padding there, but it's all tied down with this canvas. So there's a little bit of bounce because of the springs, but you end up hitting these steel rods sometimes and it really hurts. The steel beams in the ring are about 18 inches apart, but not all rings are the same. When we went to Memphis, the rods were only 12 inches apart, which meant there were more of these beams and it made the ring harder.

And all this pain, all this time spent preparing our bodies and working out, it's one of the reasons I hate when people call wrestling fake. You can't fake falling off the top rope. You can't fake hammering someone with a steel chair. You can't fake taking a bump. It's more like choreographed violence than simply saying "it's fake." When you're actually in the ring, there's a certain way of locking up and performing the moves so they look good—everything looks fluid—and a lot of that has to do with the choreography. When we lock up, my front foot is my left foot and your front foot would be you left foot. If I were to bring my right foot forward, you would drop your left foot almost like we were doing a dance move. If my right foot is forward, your right foot is forward. If my left foot is back, your left foot is back. I always found it interesting because in my head, I compared it to playing football. I was an offensive lineman, and everything about your steps is critical to making your blocks. In order for you to do your job, success has everything to do with your first step and the steps thereafter. Your footwork puts you in position to achieve your goal, and the same goes with wrestling. That's why once I got the footwork down, it made my transition to the ring so much easier. If you know you're running across the ring to hit the ropes, you know your strides and you know as you start to get closer to the ropes how you need to maneuver your body so your back or your side hits those ropes. Then, as you come off the rope, you can't have your feet in the wrong position or you're going to trip and fall. So as you hit the rope, you need to spring yourself forward so as to keep your momentum and avoid toppling over. Everything in wrestling reminds me of football because technique and footwork are key. I knew playing the O-Line that if I needed to block someone, I needed to get my feet in the right position in order to level my opponent, and that goes hand-in-hand with how it is in the ring.

For me, locking up and the footwork came quick. What took time was more of the philosophy of a match. There were certain things that were taught which you didn't know the importance of until you were actually out in front of a crowd. Dr. Tom used to teach us that when you put someone in a headlock, you never want to look down. If you look down, the crowd can't see your face. You want to look up so they can see your facial expressions or you screaming or whatever you're attempting to convey. He used to always say: "You want the guy sitting in the last row to be able to see your face." If you're in pain or pissed off, you want that guy to be able to see it just as if he were sitting in the front row.

Edge was one of my biggest supporters from the beginning. He would pull me aside after a match and I didn't even have to ask. He was always there to help. And what's funny is, the first few times he did it, he would grab me and say, "Pete, I was watching your match," and I figure he's just going to start busting my balls. But then he started breaking down my match and was really trying to help. He would be like, "When you hit the ground, why did you then do X, Y, and Z?" He would explain the right and wrong ways to do things, and that to me was the education I needed. I knew I could get the moves down, I knew I had the athleticism, but what I didn't have was the psychology behind the moves and the reason why different things were done, and that's what Edge helped me with. It was a complete team atmosphere, and once people realized that we were going to be around more than a couple of weeks, everyone really started to step up and try to help. One of the keys Edge helped me with was when to use certain moves and why you used them, and understanding that mentality is the difference between someone who lasts a month in the WWE and someone who has a full career. It's about getting that crowd to either love you or hate you. Either way, it's drawing out that passion behind the fans that will make your career.

Dr. Tom understood that we were green as hell, but he was great at knowing how to push us and how to work with us to get the most out of Rodney and me. He would send us to the ring and we would start with stretches. Dr. Tom would stretch and he'd moan like everything in his body hurt. He'd ask us how things were going then incorporate whatever we needed in our training so that we knew the moves we had to perform and take for the following week. It wasn't like going to the Power Plant or some other wrestling school where you're taking a class alongside a roomful of students. These were private lessons with one of the best trainers in the business, and it really helped speed up our careers. The more time we spent with him, the more valuable we became in the ring. We'd lock up, work on our footwork, work on some chain wrestling where you'd put someone in an arm bar, reverse out of that, then reverse out of the next move. For every move there's a reaction and a counter move, and that's a lot of what we worked on until we graduated to taking bumps, headlock takeovers, and the more basic moves. But I remember thinking that the more we learned, the more addicting it became and all I wanted to do was wrestle. I never wanted to leave the ring. I wanted to learn more, and it was definitely an amazing time because these were all the moves I saw as a kid, so while I had my own judgment on how they would work, I really had no clue. I was dead wrong about how so many moves actually worked, but I loved gaining the knowledge while on the inside of the business. To me, it was just so special to learn the ins and outs of what really went on inside the ring and how the moves were really pulled off. You might think you know by watching TV, but trust me, a lot more goes into every move than you might think.

One of the moves I was wrong about, of all thing, was the arm drag. When we were first learning, I had so many problems. As you're falling backwards, it's like a 45-degree angle where you grab your opponent under his armpit while twisting your body. I still can't do one to this day. My mind and my body just wouldn't react together. So Dr. Tom said, "Just don't do the arm drag. You don't see Stone Cold doing an arm drag. Not everyone needs to do one." However, giving an arm drag and taking one are two different things. They're completely different motions. I had no problem getting arm dragged, but doing one myself was a lot tougher than I would have originally thought. The other move I just couldn't get the grasp of was dropping an elbow. For some reason, my hips are bad (old football injury), and every time I'd go to drop an elbow—you're supposed to land on your side, but my hips couldn't take it—so I had to drop elbows almost like the Rock did, landing on my back. That's the only way I could drop an elbow without my hips killing me.

Besides my moves in the ring, the other aspect of the business I really worked on were my facial expressions, especially when someone like Shane was talking in the ring. Was I supposed to look surprised, happy, angry? You don't want it to look forced, but whatever point he is trying to get across, it's like a supporting actor in a movie: you need to help draw out that emotion from the audience. You can't just stand there and look like an oaf. It's funny how things work and how you constantly need to know everything that's happening around you because you never know what will make it on camera.

Chapter 6

Loser Leaves Town

We traveled and trained on that hectic schedule for about two months until we started to feud with Gerald Brisco and Pat Patterson over them being fired from the Corporation. In the storyline, Shane had canned them, so during *Raw* on May 3, 1999, Vince told the Stooges to go down and kick our ass for revenge. Pat Patterson pulled out his belt and started whipping me on national TV. He was pretty stiff with it, but thankfully I had my sweater on. Don't get me wrong, it didn't feel good, but it would've been a lot worse if I wasn't wearing that sweater vest (preppy clothes for the win!). Which is funny, because not only did those vests draw immediate heat and give us a signature look that people still remember and talk about, but boy did they help prevent pain and injuries, especially when it came to chest chops and moments like this with the belt. That was the same night the Rock and Stone Cold fought in a lumberjack match with the Corporation serving as lumberjacks outside the ring. The rules of a lumberjack match are that any time one of those guys got thrown out of the ring, we were to throw them back in. In this instance, however, the match turned into an all-out brawl. At one point the Corporation is beating on Stone Cold then, out of nowhere (and to my surprise), he jumps up and shoots on me, hitting me full force like a football tackle. It's like he was playing defensive line, and knocked me down while everyone else jumped back on top of him. I rolled out of the ring and was like, "Whoa!" That totally wasn't planned, but for a fan, you always dream of being in the ring with someone like Stone Cold Steve Austin, and here he is shooting on me and taking me out. It was awesome. I loved it.

That set up a Loser Leaves Town match against Brisco and Patterson. When I heard about the match, I thought for sure that this was going to be the end of our run; the end of the Mean Street Posse. It was pretty heartbreaking that after all the work we had been putting in, we were going to be sent packing by the Stooges of all people.

According to the storyline, the loser of the match would be kicked out of the WWE. And we knew when we got to the building that we were losing. It was disappointing because after they brought Rodney and me back after WrestleMania, every night we'd get off work and meet at the WWE studio to learn how to wrestle. When we were initially brought in and thrown on television, we had zero training. There was no wrestling school, no NXT, no lessons on what to do. We might be the only team ever put on *Raw* in that type of role with basically no training, but we were trying our best to catch-up. But Vince had the balls to put two kids who he knew with athletic backgrounds in the ring with the best athletes in the business and not kill ourselves, while at the same time put the guy over who we were facing, whether it was Brisco and Patterson or the Rock and Stone Cold. We had to learn on the fly. And I was 285 pounds. Sure, I was working out, but working out to be a wrestler is on a completely different level. You need to lift, you need to do cardio . . . and trust me, by looking at my pictures it's pretty obvious that I'm no Ravishing Rick Rude. I'm somewhere between Mick Foley and Prince Albert. I was heavy. I'm a former offensive lineman. So I had to start changing my body, changing my look. But then all of a sudden, during that process, we lose the Loser Leaves Town match and that's it. We didn't have a guaranteed deal. We didn't have a contract. We were told to show up, so we showed up. Funny thing is, the match ended up being one of the highest rated segments in *Raw* history. The crowd went crazy when Brisco and Patterson were kicking our asses. We might not have been trained wrestlers, but we knew how to make getting our butts beat look pretty damn good.

Before the match began, which aired the week after our *Raw* beating, the four of us went over every aspect in detail inside the ring a few hours before the show started. We went over the basics of what they were going to do and I remember Pat Patterson took me over toward the barricade and told me how he was going to throw me into the crowd. I was trying to think of how I could make this look good, so I thought I'd hit the wall, flip over the barricade, and land flat on my back. But there's no padding on the other side of that wall. It's cement. So it's one of those things where you have your adrenaline going, and it's going pretty well, so the back pain might not happen when you land, but by the time you get back to the hotel, you're not only going to hurt like hell, you're going to feel it for days.

We'd had a bunch of matches with Brisco and Patterson, so we knew each other really well and it got to the point where they were beating us up so much that Brisco put his hand over my mouth and nose to where I couldn't breathe, and he was using his forearm and the weight of his body to where I was unable to move. He's got me so tied up that he's laughing during the match. And I was getting so frustrated, but we were told before the match, "Hey, these are old guys, be careful, don't hit them. Just make it look good." If you go back and watch the Loser Leaves Town match, you'll see that we hardly got in any offense at all. It was mainly us getting our ass kicked by these two old guys. I think we had a double clothesline on Brisco, but that was it. We never hit Pat because he was too worried about getting hurt, but everything seemed to work out. They didn't get beat up, we did, but that's what everyone wanted to see. They were a little rough with us and their moves were a little snug, but it was all part of paying our dues.

It's funny because I saw Brisco in 2008, the night he got inducted into the Hall of Fame in Orlando, and I couldn't wait to walk up and talk to him. He saw me from about 20 feet away and came running over and gave me a hug and whispered, "We still have the record for the highest rating." I couldn't stop thanking him for everything he'd done to help. I knew they were a little leery working with us at first because of how green we were, but they took a chance because they knew the heat we were getting and realized we weren't just there to ride Shane's coat tails—that we really wanted to be wrestlers—so they gave us a shot in the ring. They knew the match could be huge, and it ended up being so much bigger than any of us ever imagined.

When you're in the ring with someone and they're green, you do get nervous. But to be completely honest, it was probably worse (and more worrisome) for us. Pat had been doing this for years, but he was retired, he was over the hill, so for him to wrestle us was a big chance to take with his health. So many things could have gone wrong, from landing incorrectly to tripping to even just blowing out your knee, so I don't blame him for being nervous. He had every right to feel that way.

I remember when they eventually sent us to Memphis, Tennessee, and they would put us in the ring against guys who were even greener than us. And the rule of thumb is that everyone gets three strikes. What I mean by that is, when you're in the ring with someone and they go to throw you a wrestling punch—where they bring it to the side of your jaw then break their wrist in order to make that noise or that slap—but instead they give you a stiff punch, that's strike one. I was wrestling in Memphis one time and this guy hit me with a real punch. I gave him back a working punch, and he returned with another real punch. Strike two. I gave him a working punch and, again, he hit me with a third real punch. Instead of giving him another working punch, I reached back and hit him square between the eyes, so hard I broke his nose. They call that giving you a receipt. When we went backstage, Terry Golden who was in charge in Memphis asked me what happened. This kid's nose was bleeding all over and he was bitching and moaning and crying, just like what Bradshaw was waiting for me to do when he hit me with that steel chair. But I told Terry, "We were going toe-to-toe in the ring. I threw three working punches, he threw three real punches, so he got a receipt." Terry looked at him and said:

"Kid, you just got a receipt. Consider it a lesson." That's how the business works, and that's how Brisco and Patterson treated us in the ring. They were there to entertain, but they were also there to help teach us how to perform in front of a crowd, and if we screwed up, they were ready to give us our receipt.

Luckily for us, though, no receipt was needed, even for us green guys. Shane tipped us off to the dos and don'ts of wrestling before we started, so we knew what to do and what not to do from the moment we arrived at the arena to stepping inside the ring to the when we left and headed off to the next city. He pulled us aside and said, "Listen, when you go into a locker room, you make sure you shake everybody's hand. And when you leave at the end of the night, you walk around and shake everybody's hand." It's all about being polite and showing respect to every single person in that locker room. Because if you don't show that respect to people, not only will they not respect you back, but they'll hurt you in that ring. Even the way you shake someone's hand is very important. If I'm wrestling you that night and go up to you and squeeze your hand really hard, you're going to say something along the lines of, "I hope you don't wrestle the way you shake hands." It's an unwritten rule where, if I shake a hand and I squeeze it, that means I don't know how to work in the ring. If I shake your hand and I have my hand wrapped tight around yours but I'm not squeezing it, that shows I know how to work and I'm going to keep you safe in the ring.

Anyway, we lost the Loser Leaves Town match, and we went back to sitting at home watching *Raw* on TV like everyone else, figuring that was the end of the line. We went back to our regular jobs and, to be honest, it was really a downer moving on from staring on TV one night to working 9–5 the following week. But I have to say, because of our past relationship with Shane, we were always treated differently by Vince than the rest of the roster. So after the Loser Leaves Town match, Vince said something that I'll always remember, and it was something I thought about a lot as I went back to work. Vince never wanted to show us any favoritism in the locker room because it would've been like feeding the sharks, so if anything, he was always really hard on us. But I remember after we lost the match to Brisco and Patterson, we got a phone call and it was Shane, but Vince was in the car. Shane tells us, "Hey, great job tonight. You guys really made the match work. We can't wait to see what the ratings will be." Then he tells us that somebody else wants to say something, and Vince gets on the phone. He says, "I'm proud of you. I see how hard you guys are working and how you're trying your best out there, and I just wanted to let you know how much we appreciate what you've done." He actually said thank you and that he was proud of us, and I can still hear him saying it in my head. It's an amazing feeling to know that someone you have that much respect for, someone you've looked at as a father figure, recognized all the hard work you put in. Rodney and I used to travel all over together, and we always talked about how we wanted to make this work, not only for us, but for the McMahons. We never wanted to let them down. We were Shane's buddies, but we didn't want to go out there and be the weak link. We didn't want to look like a couple of assholes who were just out there to get paid because they were friends of the boss's son. So it just meant the world to us that Vince was proud of what we had become. We never wanted to screw things up or get anyone hurt or have anyone not respect us. You are always looking for respect in this industry, and we were always trying to improve. But after we lost the Loser Leaves Town match, it looked like our run was finally over.

Super Soakers

During the Brisco/Patterson feud, we were working house shows so we could practice taking bumps in front of a live crowd. In this one loop, we were going to Tampa for a Saturday show, and we had to be there extra early because they wanted us to film a Super Soaker commercial. It was Rodney and myself with Brisco and Patterson. In the commercial, Rodney and I had Super Soakers in our hands and sunglasses on. Brisco and Patterson were then supposed to drive up in a golf cart and tell us to leave the arena. We were told to shoot Brisco and Patterson with the Super Soakers, and after we shot them, they were supposed to get out and run away. Before we start filming, Pat specifically said, "Whatever you do, don't shoot me in the face, and most of all, don't shoot me in the crotch." The script called for me to shoot him in the stomach, and I remember saying, "No way I'm sticking to this script." So I shot him in the groin with my first shot, and they called for another take. So I shot him in the groin again. We had a blast. It was so much fun working with those guys. They never gave us any offense in our matches, so this was my way of getting back at them. And Pat was getting pissed, but the more I kept doing it, the funnier it got. And by the end even Pat was laughing about it. It was hot as hell out there, but we all had a real good time. This was one of those moments where you don't know how good you've got it until it's gone. Every week, we were on TV, sometimes three or four times in a night, and every week we were doing something different, something fun, and this was our job. What a great time in my life. Unbelievable.

Chapter 7

Get the Posse Back Together

It was May 23, 1999, and Rodney had come over to watch the latest pay-per-view, Over the Edge. I was always a fan of Owen Hart and his Blue Blazer gimmick, but on this night, we were watching from home like everyone else when tragedy struck and he fell from the balcony to his death. Luckily, his fall didn't make the broadcast, but Rodney and I immediately knew that something was wrong. The lights went out when Owen was supposed to be lowered into the ring and by the look on the faces of the announcers you knew this wasn't a work—this was as real as it gets. Just two weeks earlier, we were sitting down with Owen eating breakfast and he was talking about his family. You could just tell how much he loved them by the way he gushed. Then in a flash, he was gone. They showed Jerry Lawler moments after Owen had fallen. He was so pale, looking like he was about to throw up. And I remember talking to Jerry about it a year later when we were on a flight together to Memphis. We were just shooting the shit and I asked him, "In all your years, what's the worst thing you've ever seen in the ring?" He didn't even hesitate. He just said, "Owen Hart. I watched him fall to his death. I saw him hit the turnbuckle and I saw him not move. I knew it was real bad." Hearing that just broke his heart, and his death also broke the heart of everyone who knew and loved Owen, whether you were a friend or a fan.

But, like I said, we were still at home at this time, and I was back at work, finally getting everything back to normal with my bosses. I told them that my wrestling career was over, and I think they were relieved. When I was on the road with WWE, there wasn't anyone around to make first-hand decisions in case something went wrong (like when a trailer's lights went out or got flooded). I always had my phone with me to take care of business, but after a while my bosses weren't too happy about me taking off every week to go on the road and skipping out on what needed to be handled from their end. They had their own goals and needed me to be in a certain place at a certain time, but I just couldn't do it. At first, it was cool that I was on TV, but then it became, "Wow, he's not going to be at work again?!" It got pretty old with my bosses, so by the time I told them my wrestling career was through, they were relieved because they were almost at their limit. Then again, even when I was at work, my mind was in the ring. Sure, I would still do my job, but all I could think about was wrestling. It was a dream I had back as a little kid, and it was suddenly coming true, even if I still had to have a 9-to-5 to support myself.

Before I had worked behind the camera, but now that I was in front of the camera, I found out you're treated a whole lot differently. I was only twenty-eight years old, so it was an easy decision. I had to follow my dreams. I had to take that chance to be on *Raw* as a member of the Posse, even if it only lasted a few months. It was worth it, even if they were going to fire me.

Little did I know, Shane was going to come calling one last time.

"Pete, I need to see you and Rodney in my office. I need to talk to you guys about something."

So we head over to his office and Shane walks up to us and throws over those 10x13 sized envelopes. They were both thick as hell and I remember catching the envelope and looking inside. That's when Shane told us, "We want to sign you both to three, one-year deals." The Mean Street Posse was officially on the WWE roster.

I couldn't believe it. But it's not like we were millionaires or anything. People see you on TV and they think you're rich, but we weren't even making six figures. I think that first year, our deal was for about $90K, but that doesn't include hotels or rental cars or anything like that. So the good news is, you're on the roster, but the bad news is, it's a struggle to stay there, even if it is your dream. (I still have my copy of the contract in my safe at home because of how much I cherish it. I will look at it from time to time and it always reminds me of how elated I was when we received it.)

Not to mention, the contracts weren't guaranteed. After the first year, it was up to the office whether or not they would sign the second one-year contract. That's just how it was. We worked on three, one-year deals. But I remember the day it happened, Rodney and I left Shane's office and were all fired up to be back. We missed every second that we were away. We missed performing, we missed the guys, we missed being the Mean Street Posse. So here we were, in the parking lot of Titan Towers and I just let out a scream. I couldn't believe our careers weren't over. We were officially written off the script, but now we were getting our shot to not only come back, but actually be official members of the roster. It was an amazing feeling.

The night of June 7, 1999, is when WWE brought back the Mean Street Posse after we were forced to "leave town." That was the same night Stone Cold was named CEO by Linda McMahon. It had already been revealed that Vince was the Higher Power, and how he used his power to get even with Stone Cold. Vince became the ultimate heel by showing he would even have his own daughter abducted if it meant getting to Austin. Linda, who was CEO at the time, said she was stepping down, but that she was announcing a successor, and it was Stone Cold. Austin then came out with a pair of jeans on, a t-shirt, and a tie over his t-shirt. He also had a clip board and a couple cans of beer, and the fans ate it up like they did for just about anything Austin did back then. From the stage, he made all of these declarations, including making Shane wrestle both X-Pac and Kane. During this match, there were two guys in the front row: one was wearing a Kane mask and the other was wearing a Mick Foley Halloween mask, as well as ridiculous wigs. It just happened to be Rodney and me.

We were cheering but wearing sweater vests, so I don't know how people didn't know it was us. Some fans didn't seem to realize what was going on, which was funny in itself. But then at one point, we interfered in the match in order to help Shane.

Nobody seemed to realize what was going on until Rodney and I took off our masks while walking up the ramp. The place went nuts and we were screaming like mad, only for Brisco and Patterson to jump us from behind and throw us into the ring. Rodney then got choke slammed by Kane, and then they put him in the corner and he received a Bronco Buster from X-Pac. After that, I ate a spin kick from X-Pac and a Tombstone from Kane. This was the first Tombstone I ever took and I remember during practice prior to the show, Shane told me that when he puts you up there, make sure you don't fall with your head lower than Kane's knees. I didn't want to end up breaking my neck like Austin did in the piledriver he took against Owen Hart years earlier. So when Kane picked me up, I remember squeezing the shit out of him so my body didn't slip when he did the move. I was bear hugging his waist so tight because all I kept thinking was, "don't break my neck, don't break my neck." But when it was over, I was happy as hell. Not only did I survive, bones intact, but it was another famous finishing move that I had taken on live TV. Another one under my belt.

One week later, it was Mideon and Viscera's turn to face Brisco and Patterson on *Raw*. As Mideon and Viscera walked down to the ring, we jumped out of the crowd again and attacked Brisco and Patterson from behind. It was just about us getting heat, and that's a credit to Vince Russo, who at the time was the head writer of *Raw* and the genius behind the Attitude Era. He always made sure that guys up and down the card, even if you didn't have a match, were on the show and extending your feud and storyline. If you watch the product today, they cut a storyline short too often or just forget about them all together and move on to something else. Back in the Attitude Era, Russo really had his finger on what was happening throughout the show, and one storyline really flowed on to the next up and down the card. And that's what this one did. Our storyline with Brisco and Patterson started in May, and it didn't end until they got even with us at SummerSlam during the end of our match.

Before that, though, there was a new addition to the Posse, one that I hoped would take us to the next level. On June 21, it was Shane and Vince versus Brisco and Patterson. But, as usual, all hell broke loose. Ken Shamrock ran down and suplexed Shane. Then after Vince had run backstage, Shamrock left the ring and followed him. That left Brisco and Patterson with Shane, so that was the cue for the Mean Street Posse to come running out through the crowd (again) and save the day. I always loved running in through the crowd because it's something the fans didn't expect. You'd see the excitement in their eyes and they'd start yelling in a way that just didn't happen when you came down the ramp. The element of surprise was always electric. Security would show up and tell people to stay in their seat, then we'd run through the tunnel and jump the railing to get into the ring. We couldn't be seen right away, otherwise it would cause a stir and the crowd wouldn't watch the match, so it's one of those things you have to time perfectly in order to get it over. What made this night special, however, is that Joey Abs was introduced as the newest member of the Posse. Joey is Jason Ahrndt, and he was added to the Mean Street Posse in order to give us one guy who could actually work matches and not hurt himself or others. The WWE decided that if they were going to bring us back on TV, we needed someone who could actually work. The original plan was to bring in this guy named Steve Bradley, but he had gotten mononucleosis right before he got called up from Memphis, so the next man up was Jason Ahrndt. They gave Jason the name Joey Abs, which came from a close friend of ours named

Joey Abbazia. Abs had been working down in North Carolina for Omega, an organization made famous by the Hardy Boyz. He had done dark matches in the past for the WWE under the name Venom, so they knew he could work. At that time, Abs had been just offered a deal by ECW because Tommy Dreamer loved the way he worked and wanted to make him a huge star. They actually had a character lined up for him and everything, but right before he started, Jim Ross gave Jason a call and offered him a position in the Mean Street Posse. From what I've been told, Jason got the call to go to the number one company, and he passed on his ECW character to join us. Whether or not that was the best decision long-term, we'll never know, but if it wasn't for Steve Bradley being sick, he would've made it into WWE and Jason might have went on to become a big-time player in ECW. It's great the way the pieces fell, though, because Abs turned out to be one of my best friends, and we never would've had the chance to be this close if Bradley hadn't been sick. Abs is like a brother to me, so I feel bad for saying it, but it worked out for everyone that Steve got sick.

* * *

In the new and improved Mean Street Posse, Abs became the muscle, while Rodney and I would cause the chaos. That was the plan, as we were still learning how to wrestle. But at least this way we could stay on TV while continuing to work on our skills behind the scenes. It's funny, though, because when Abs first joined, the WWE didn't want him to speak. Abs had a southern accent (originally from Carthage, North Carolina), which didn't really fit with the boys from Greenwich, but it didn't matter because Abs was awesome right from the start. The three of us all clicked right from the moment he joined the group, and it's one of those things where it's strange to even think of the Mean Street Posse without him. We began traveling together and he was pretty much a screwball like the rest of us. The first loop of towns the three of us rode together with Abs in the back seat. Smash Mouth had just released the single "All-Star," and he loved that song. He started belting out the lyrics at the top of his lungs. I looked at Rodney, we were both smiling and I said to him, "Abs is gonna fit in with us perfectly, he's as fucked up as we are!"

Another plus was that he knew the business and had seen it all. He would tell us stories about small-time promoters ripping him off and would explain the business from a different perspective. All it did was make me appreciate my opportunity even more and aware of my surroundings. He would help Rodney and me with training and teach us the philosophy of a match. Not only was he helping us, he was helping himself. The better we became, the more job security for him. As time went on, we started "getting it" and were able to work matches at a higher level.

On June 28, the following week, there was a thing called GTV. It was this weird black-and-white video that would catch something scandalous and show it on the Titantron. It was never really explained who was behind it (Goldust?), but it would catch embarrassing stuff behind the scenes like Al Snow picking his nose then eating it or something along those lines. On this particular episode, GTV showed Test and Stephanie walking out of a hotel, and Test goes to open the car door for her and they start kissing.

Later in the show, Terry Taylor was doing an interview backstage with Test when Shane and the three Posse members step up. Before you know it, Shane spears Test into the set, then all of these long metal pipes go crashing to the floor to cause this huge noise during the mêlée. And it's funny because whenever there's a brawl backstage, you'll notice these 8-foot long pipes are always leaning against something where the fight ends up, and they always go bouncing to the floor. These things make the loudest noises when they fall and hit each other, and you'll notice this large, sharp metallic sound whenever they land, and it just helps add to the chaos of backstage fights. Just a fun thing to look out for next time you see a backstage brawl.

We were in North Carolina that night, and as we were leaving the show we got invited by Shane to join him and Vince and a bunch of production people to eat at a place called Vinnie's Steakhouse. It was named after Vince McMahon and it was Vince's best friend who owned the steakhouse. So we went in there and had an amazing steak with all the sides and beer—we all just went to town. At the same time, we got to see Vince around one of his best friends growing up and how they interacted, and that was cool because it was rare to see that side of Vince, even for us, and we knew him for what seemed like forever.

The next night we were flying back to Stamford, and the office had Abs come with us so he could get the chemistry down and help us on our wrestle technique. We would work matches, we would switch up working tag matches with Rodney and me versus Abs and Dr. Tom Pritchard, or me and Abs vs. Rodney and Tom. In the process of working with each other, you get to know more about the other person and a bond starts to grow. I even brought Abs home for one of my mom's famous Italian dinners. My mom always made pasta at her house with homemade meatballs, and we've had some big athletes eat at our house like Steve Young and Brian Kozlowski (of the New York Giants), so she loves her resume of who she's cooked for, and Abs is right up there among her favorites. But it was great because he stayed with us for a week, and we'd work out, train in the ring, eat, then go out and grab a few drinks at night. It built a bond that made us stronger as a group and gel quicker as a team. Even though Abs was this southern guy and we were from the northeast, we still had a lot in common. We really became a close unit.

* * *

Raw: July 5, 1999

After the GTV video, the storyline went that Test was dating Stephanie (not in real life, despite the rumors), and so Test had to work a match with Joey Abs. During the match, Shane drags Stephanie down the ramp, and she's trying to resist, and the whole distraction of Shane and Stephanie causes Test to stop beating on Abs. Test starts yelling at Shane to let her go, which enables Rodney and I to once again jump in from the crowd and the three of us start beating on Test. Shane held Stephanie and forced her to watch as he yelled, "See what happens?" He didn't want Test and Stephanie to have a relationship, and now Test had to pay. This helped make us serious heels now because we were standing in the way of "true love." Everyone feeling bad for them just added more heat for us.

On the following week of *Raw*, GTV strikes again, only this time Stephanie is leaning up against the wall and Abs is trying to talk to her. You find out that Stephanie and Abs dated at one point. GTV shows Abs trying to make up with her, and then later that night Test had to face the entire Posse in a match, only one at a time. This is after we jumped him during his match with Mr. Ass on *Sunday Night Heat* the previous night.

We enter and, at the top of the stage did Rock-Paper-Scissors to see who would go first, and I won.

Test beat the shit out of me, giving me the big boot on the ramp and throwing me into the stairs, which I hit with my right leg, and flipped over the top. When I took the bump, my right femur popped out of my hip. But when you're in the middle of a match, you have so much adrenaline surging through your body that you just keep going. So I take that bump, then Test jumps on me and then throws me over the Spanish announcers table, rolling off onto the chairs then the ground beneath me. Test throws me in the ring and goes to the top rope and gives me a flying elbow. He pinned me and I was eliminated, then he pinned Rodney.

After turning the table on Abs, who had been controlling the match, Shane came out and took Test's knee out. After Test started beating on Shane, Steve Blackman came out to defend Shane, which was shortly followed by Ken Shamrock coming after Blackman. So with Test down we all run back into the ring and start beating on him.

By this time my femur popped back into my hip and we're all doing our thing when a referee runs to the ring and grabs Shane from behind. Shane throws an elbow to get him off, then Stephanie runs down and bear hugs Shane from behind. Shane, not knowing it was his sister, throws another back elbow and connects with Stephanie in the side of the head. Shane is worried, yelling we need to get help, and then Shane carries her to the back as the show goes off the air.

On the next week of *Raw*, the Mean Street Posse is in the ring and we call Stephanie down to apologize. After Shane says he's sorry, he hands the microphone to Joey Abs who says he forgives her for going out with Test and that he'd still take her back. This just brings more heat on us, and then she explains how it was only one date with Abs and she only did it as a favor to Shane, but now she wants all of us out of her life.

That pissed off Test, so he goes out the following week and gets his revenge on us. He threw me into some barriers backstage, and I remember when we were planning this bump I wanted there to be a reason why my character was going to stay down on the ground so long during the segment. So I went up to Taker and I asked him if I should take this bump by throwing my body sideways into the barrier. I wanted to earn respect with the boys, I wanted to make it look good, and I wanted people at home to be like, "Oh man, Pete Gas took one hell of a bump." So I ask Taker, "Would you take a bump sideways like that?" and he goes, "I wouldn't, but go for it." So I did it, and it didn't hurt, and it actually looked pretty decent. Then Test picked up a metal pipe and started beating me in the ribs.

That was the last time I was on television until SummerSlam because, according to the story, I had internal injuries and wasn't allowed to compete (from the Test beating). So in the following weeks, he supposedly broke Rodney's arm, then broke Joey Abs's leg. Which brings us to SummerSlam, August 22, 1999, and one of the best matches I've ever been a part of.

Chapter 8

Passing the Test

Leading up to SummerSlam 1999, we were a pain in the ass to Test onscreen, jumping him at every chance and driving his character nuts. But off screen, Test hated us just as much. The guy couldn't stand us. He didn't even have to say a word, but backstage, I don't know if he was trying to make a name for himself or what, but he would constantly give us these dirty looks. In the ring he was giving stiff kicks where he'd give me the big boot, but he was putting it in my throat. And then he'd go to punch me, and his punches were always stiff. So that led to the two of us having a strong dislike for each other from the beginning.

I was there to put him over, but all he was doing was acting like a douche, and when you start hitting people for real, that's when you have to man up and do something. If you don't stand up for yourself in the ring and answer with a receipt, the boys in the back smell the blood in the water and they're going to take advantage of you every time. You have to fight back. There are parts of the match where you're ad-libbing out there, and if you don't fight back and get yours, your character looks weak. And with Test not liking us—and me specifically—he just wanted to make us look like shit out there. He didn't appreciate the push we were getting and felt the only reason we were on TV was because we were Shane's friends.

Going back and watching footage of our matches, I can see the look on my face and how pissed I was during certain spots because he'd just hit me with a stiff shot. I was actually in there yelling at him in the ring, telling him if he kept it up, I was going to give him a fucking receipt, meaning that if he hit me stiff, I'd hit him stiff right back. Eventually, though, we had the Summer-Slam match with Test, and Shane as the perfectionist wanted to steal the show with his match. He always wanted to do something over the top so people were talking about him when the event ended—and he usually did. So for SummerSlam he had a little bit of everything in that match. He had different types of hardcore stuff where he made us go out and buy a mailbox and paint it with dollar signs and write "Mean Street Posse" on it. We actually went to a store on Greenwich Ave. and bought as many props as we could just so he could hit Test with them. He even hit Test with a big picture of the Mean Street Posse.

But leading up to the match, Shane wanted to go over every aspect of the match just so we had it down perfect. We ended up spending two or three days together going over this match, and by that time, we had every spot down. We ran every move over and over and over again until we had it down exactly the way Shane wanted.

After our last day of practice, Shane took us to Morton's Steakhouse and you could tell there was a change in Test's demeanor. He finally had some respect for what we were doing out there. And the feeling was mutual. All five of us had a goal in mind that we were going to put on an amazing match and, in a lot of people's minds, that match stole the show. There was just so much going on, from the weapons to the couch in the front row for the Mean Street Posse to my neck brace to the casts that Rodney and Joey Abs had, and there were just all these twists and turns and false finishes . . . and the crowd popped with every one of them. And I think everybody thought Test was going to lose that night, but he fought off every one of us. And just when we were going back to save Shane that one last time, Brisco and Patterson run down, preventing us from getting to Test one last time and beat the shit out of us and knock us out with our own street signs.

From that point on, not only did the mutual respect level between Test and I grow, but we actually became very, very close. Before his death, we still talked or texted to break each other's balls about different things. I remember one time back in 2004 when we were on the phone and I asked, "Hey Test, have you seen our SummerSlam match lately?" I was in the WWE offices, so I grabbed some extra DVDs of the show and mailed him a copy and a couple days later he called and couldn't thank me enough, not only for sending him the DVD but that he realized and appreciated how much we put him over and helped put him on the map. That match and storyline helped springboard his career and it was big for him. Years later, there we were, we were both out of WWE, and it was nice to hear him say how much that match and our time together meant to him.

It's funny, because after SummerSlam we went from despising each other to actually traveling together on the road. In one car, it would be the Mean Street Posse and in the other car it would be Prince Albert, Val Venis, and Test. We would drive from city to city together, find someplace to eat along the way, then head to the hotel in the next town. In the morning we'd all hit the gym and then head to the arena. We built a camaraderie that comes with traveling together thousands of miles every week, and if it wasn't for that match at SummerSlam, I don't think we would have ever had that. We probably would've hated each other forever. Test just had that cocky arrogance to him and if you weren't a part of his inner circle, he just wasn't the kind of guy who would open up to you.

Around ten days prior to him passing away—and I'll never forget—it was a Tuesday and I called Test to shoot the shit. I asked him what he was up to, and he told me he was getting ready to do a tour in Europe. He told me how he does these tours every couple of months and it's really good money, then asked if I wanted to do one with him some time. "I'll even put you over."

I started laughing and I told him, "You don't put anybody over."

Cracking up, he said, "You're right, I was bullshitting. But seriously, I'll talk to the promoter and get you on the show."

I told him how it would be an honor to work with him again and how much fun it would be to go around Europe together. But then it happened.

Like I said, ten days later, I woke up and was getting ready to help a buddy of mine move some furniture into his house.

I'm an early riser, so I got up, walked the dog, then when I got home, I was drinking a protein shake and decided to see what was going on in the wrestling dirt sheets. I looked and there was a story that Andrew Martin, Test, was found dead, but the news wasn't confirmed. So I picked up the phone and I called him right away. It went to his voicemail and through tears was like, "Please call me back! Please tell me you're okay!" I remember telling his voicemail, "I love you, please call me back." He meant so much to me, I just couldn't believe what had happened. I was on the wrestling site, and I just kept hitting refresh, hoping that the rumor would be shot down and that he was actually fine. I was hoping my buddy Test wasn't gone. But then an hour later they put up another story: Andrew Martin confirmed dead.

I didn't know what to do. I didn't know what to say. I called Matt Bloom (Prince Albert, Tensai) and we both couldn't believe that our friend was really gone. That's one thing about this business that is very difficult. I don't have an addictive personality. I've seen what has happened to so many of my friends, and I'm afraid to be addicted to anything. I tried chewing tobacco but was afraid I'd getting addicted, so I quit. I've never been into drugs. I like drinking, but I don't drink too much because I never wanted to be an alcoholic.

We did so much wrestling with Crash Holly with Test, and now these guys are gone. If I go back and look at a *Raw* from 1999, there are like 10 to 12 people who are gone now, and they were young guys. You can say it was steroids, you can say it was drugs, but I think it's a combination of everything. You're out there abusing your body and putting crap into your system and the consequences are grave. Thankfully, a lot of the recreational drugs guys were taking back then are now banned from WWE. A pill that was a wrestler's best friend, a muscle relaxer called Soma is now banned, and that's great. If you get caught with it in your system now, you're suspended. And I constantly get letters from the WWE office that they will help you if you have any type of issue or addiction. They even have programs set up to help you with your financial planning. It's amazing that they do this now, because in the old days, the guys didn't make much money and they ended up pissing it all away. Now the guys are investing their money and they're not left broke and broken down in addiction when they end their careers. It's amazing what they do now for everyone.

Chapter 9

Hangin' with the Posse

On *Monday Night Raw*, the day after SummerSlam, Test calls Stephanie out to the ring, drops down to one knee, and proposes to her. Before she has a chance to answer, Shane runs down and tells her to stop, not to do it, and Stephanie ends up saying she needs some time to think. While we weren't on that episode, it was setting up the next chapter of the story.

On August 26, 1999, in Kansas City, Missouri, we were at the first episode of *SmackDown* (the pilot was in April, but the August show was the network premiere). The show began with "Commissioner" Shawn Michaels announcing a match between

Triple H and the Rock (with himself being the special guest referee). Shane then came out and announced himself as the *second* special guest referee. However, Michaels had something else up his sleeve: Shane would be unable to be the second special guest referee, as he'd be facing Mankind that evening.

But before you knew it, Rock and Mankind ran into the ring and the four guys ended up getting into a fight . . . but the Posse was not far behind. We ran down to the ring to interfere, and the Rock ends up hooking me into the Rock Bottom and the crowd literally erupts. It was such a great roar that all I could think was how great it would be to have the crowd react like that to your every move like they did for the Rock. He's a once in a lifetime performer, the Michael Jordan of the WWE, and everything he does is special.

Back in the Attitude Era, there would be hundreds of signs throughout the arena. There would be so many signs that you couldn't see the people in the crowd. It always felt like the roof was going to pop off because of all of the emotion and screaming. Girls would be flashing DX, the signs were racy ("I'd rather be in Chyna"), and I can easily understand why people would want it to go back to those times. Those shows were never dull, and that's a true testament to Vince Russo's writing. It was unbelievable how alive that crowd was. And to be hooked into the Rock Bottom, and to feel the energy in the crowd, was simply amazing. Rock also knew how to make the most of the situation. When he hooked me in the move, he paused ever so slightly so as to work the crowd into a complete frenzy. Then when he hits it, the crowd just pops.

Later that evening, Stephanie calls Test to the ring and says she's ready to give her answer: yes, she'll marry him!

So, of course, we go running down and beat Test while Shane holds Stephanie in the corner. This causes Mick Foley to run down and he ends up hitting me, Rodney, and Abs in the head with chairs. Shane flees outside the ring and Mick goes, "You and I are going to have our match right now. . . . I'll tell you what, I'll sweeten the pot. I'm gonna leave this chair that I just dented over your buddy's skulls, and I'm gonna leave it right here . . . and I'm going to let you have one shot . . . so make it a good one." Then Mick said something that still cracks me up today: "While you're thinking about it, I'll be over here hanging with the Posse." What's funny is he used to talk like that backstage, so it was cool the way he said it on TV.

* * *

At that time, Rodney and I were still trying to earn the respect of the boys. So when we were backstage before the match, I go up to Mick and I tell him, "Hey Mick, we're trying to earn some respect here, so when you hit us with these chairs, go ahead and lay it in."

> My brother took my nephew to a kid's party at the WWE restaurant years later when I was already out of wrestling, and Mick Foley was the special WWE guest. Mick was telling this story to some of the parents, and my brother went up afterward and introduced himself to Mick, and Mick said, "Your brother wanted it, he got it. I laid it in."

I don't know if Mick thought I was crazy for wanting to get smacked in the head with a chair or if he understood that we were trying to get that respect from the boys in the back, but either way, he accommodated us. What's funny, though, is we walk to the back after taking the chair shots and nobody said a word to us. So it's not like you get instant respect, but it helps build up the respect level in the wrestler's minds like, "OK, these guys are here for real. These aren't just Shane's friends trying to make a quick buck. These guys are doing their best out there in the ring," and hopefully they saw we were really improving. The longer you take the beatings and get back up, the more respect you're able to earn. You also learn an important strategy: when you're going to take a chair shot, feed them your back, not your head. Part of you wants to take the chair shot in the head so they say, "wow, this kid is tougher than we thought," but for the good of your body (and brains) you can't take those unprotected shots to the head, so I'm glad the WWE has now banned them from action.

It took about eight months in the business for the other wrestlers to realize how much we were busting our ass.

By this time I was really working hard in my training with Dr. Tom, and he told Rodney and me: "When you go home at night, start thinking of things you'd like to try out as your finishing move."

A finishing move!? Hell yeah! I've been dreaming of having a finishing move since I was a kid, and now I get to make it a reality.

Buff Bagwell used to get on the second rope, jump over his opponent while grabbing him under the chin, and have his opponent take a simple back bump, but it looked great. And that's key: not only did it look good, but everyone in the ring knows how to take a back bump so you could do it to anyone, small (Rey Mysterio Jr.) or large (Big Show).

That's what Dr. Tom told us. "When you pick a finishing move, make sure it's a move that everyone on the roster can take." You didn't want to limit yourself in case you were fighting someone too big or too small. The Rock has the People's Elbow. There isn't a single person in wrestling who can't take an elbow. Rodney decided that he was going to steal Bagwell's move but take it to the next level, and so would perform it from the top rope. Since he was up high, I told him, "Why don't you call it the High Society?" With the Mean Street Posse gimmick, it worked perfectly. For me, I just kept playing off the name Gas. I'm thinking Gas Chamber, Gas Face, Gas Mask, anything to do with Gas. So I decide I'm going to put someone in the STF (stepover toehold facelock) and call it the Gas Chamber. I never once got to use it on live television for WWE, just in Memphis, but then John Cena started using the STF and calling it the STFU, so it was never going to fly. I then moved on to the Gas Mask and started putting my hands in front of my face, and at one point, I interlocked my fingers and I thought instantly of the Full Nelson. But to me, the Gas Mask was a reverse Full Nelson, so instead of having my hands behind my opponent's head, if I reversed it, I'm face to face with my opponent and my arms are wrapped around his arms and my hands are clinched like I would if I had him in a Full Nelson. So I brought my idea to Dr. Tom and asked him what he thought, and he liked it. Then he added: "How about you do a sit down powerbomb from that position, where all you do is let go in mid-air and let him take a back bump?" God bless Dr. Tom. He was my guinea pig and we experimented with different ways to do the move, and I paid my dues on this as we were trying to figure it out.

Guys didn't initially know how to take the move, and there was one time where a guy's teeth actually went into my forehead. So here I am, doing my finishing move, and I'm the one who ended up bloody. That was during a dark match, and when I came backstage, I actually had to get stitches. While the doctor was working on me, I was getting my balls busted by everyone else. "Wasn't that *your* finishing move? How did you end up with blood?" My opponent had loose teeth and I had a bloody head, but I learned my lesson and continued to adjust the move.

Instead of having the guy straddle me in mid-air, I wanted to make it more so when I went to lift him up—it was almost like a Rock Bottom where when I jump up, both of our legs kick out at the same time, with him landing on his back and me landing on my ass. Then as we're going down, I let go enabling him to take the bump and me to be able to land on the right side so I can just roll over and get the pin. It took some time, but I was proud of it. It was something that nobody had ever done before, but it's cool to see the move live on television.

About four years after I got released, I was watching *SmackDown* on a Friday night, and Luke Gallows used the Gas Mask on TV. I just stared at the screen and kept muttering to myself, "Motherfucker just took my move!" It's not like I was using it, though. So a few years later, in 2015, I'm doing an independent show for one of the Nasty Boys, Brian Knobbs. I was getting dressed in the locker room before the show and I look over, and there's Luke Gallows. So I walk over to him and introduce myself. He was like, "Yeah, yeah, I know who you are," and we keep talking, and I'm just waiting for the right moment. Then out of nowhere I'm like, "Hey Luke, how do you like the Gas Mask?" His eyes just lit up.

He said, "I was wondering if you ever saw that. Are you mad? I hope you're not mad." So I told him, "When I first saw you do it, I was pretty upset because I worked hard to get it right." But he was like, "I love that move. It's so big, and they love it in Japan."

That made me proud, and while I was initially pissed, I said how flattered I was that my move was still being used. I mean, here's this guy who's huge in the business and he thought enough of my move that he wanted to use it. So now I think it's pretty awesome, especially when I saw him on *Raw* and looked at his clothes and saw a gas mask.

Now that I had my finisher, I needed someone to actually finish it on.

As the storyline went, back in the summer of 2000, Meat got caught cheating on Terri Runnels with Mrs. Cleavage, so the following week we come out to face Brisco, Patterson, and Test, and Terri Runnels walks out in front of us and says that she's our new manager. That she was looking for three well-educated, handsome guys to take under her wing. We jump Brisco and Patterson, but then Test runs down to the ring and absolutely lays waste to all three of us, once again helping us earn some respect with Test since we were making him look like Superman. The writing staff wanted to team us with Terri to give her something after her relationship with Meat turned sour. Meat didn't have much to say, and he never drew much of a following, so adding Terri provided an instant crowd reaction. But when she got teamed with us, it only ended up being for a month in sort of a transitional period for us all. She's an absolute sweetheart, though. She has a great mind for the business and knows a lot more than anyone ever gives her credit for. She didn't take many bumps in her day, but that doesn't mean she doesn't know the ins and outs of the business. I mean, she was with the company for at least fifteen years. And she would actually give us some great suggestions when we'd be going over the match beforehand backstage. She didn't do house shows with us, but it was great to be able to pick her brain until they pawned us off on the British Bulldog about a month later.

Chapter 10

The Big Race

The next week on *SmackDown*, we were told by Shane to leave Stephanie and Test alone, but of course we didn't listen. So anytime we'd jump Test, Shane would run down to help Test out.

For example, Test and Abs had a match in Anaheim, Test beats Abs, we beat down Test after the match, and then Shane runs down and attacks us, instantly becoming a huge babyface. I always loved when the roles would reverse like that as the crowd always eats it up. In a matter of seconds, all that heat you had as a heel turns to instant love from the fans, and it's moments like that which are truly memorable.

Personally, I love when a babyface turns heel the most. Two faces will be in the ring and the crowd is loving them, then one of the faces screws over the other and next thing you know he's the most hated man in the building. Instant heel heat with the flip of a switch.

This leads to a whole new angle. Our characters didn't want to let it go, we didn't want to let Stephanie leave with Test, so this led to even more matches between the Posse and Brisco/Patterson. So on *SmackDown* (September 16), what happened was that, per the storyline, the referees went on strike. So during a Shane vs. Abs match, Jerry Brisco came down as the referee. He was about to do the three count on Abs, so I pulled him out of the ring and started beating on him. But then Patterson runs down to make the count, and Rodney hits him. Stasiak (Meat) then came out and gave the three count for Shane to finally beat Abs.

> On October 7, we were in Long Island for *SmackDown*, which is usually great to be so close to home, but it was a rough week as Gorilla Monsoon had passed away the day before. We used to go to Shane's house as kids for the McMahon's Christmas parties. Classy Freddie Blassie dressed up as Santa one year, and Rodney and I actually sat on his lap as college students fooling around and pretending to tell him what we wanted for Christmas. Gorilla Monsoon would always be at all of these Christmas parties, and what was amazing is that we'd all go out drinking afterwards.

We loved Gorilla, he was just a great guy. In fact, he was the inventor of the word "kayfabe" (portrayal of staged wrestling events as real) and had it as his license plate. That's my license plate in the state of New York, except instead of the b, I have the number 8, and having that word on my car is a tribute to this great man. He was such a huge influence on the business. The room behind the Titantron is called the Gorilla position because of him. What's funny is Gorilla used to go to school with my high school football coach, so we used to hear stories about him at practice, then we'd go to these parties and hear his version of the same stories. It was classic. Gorilla lost a lot of weight later in life due to the cancer, and it was sad to see, but he is still one of the nicest guys I've ever met.

* * *

During an episode of *Raw* on November 1, Mosh and Thrasher were facing the Dudley Boyz. After Thrasher pinned Bubba Ray Dudley for the victory, we slide in and all start fighting each other to begin a three-team feud.

Then we find out that, later that weekend, we were going to go work an independent show against the Dudley Boyz. It would be a Saturday night match in Jersey, and then we were going straight back to TV. The Dudley Boyz had a reputation for being pretty stiff in the ring, especially with rookies. Mosh really looked out for us, and even to this day he's a really good friend of mine. He pulled the Dudley Boyz aside before the match and said, "These guys are green. If they fuck up, don't beat the shit out of them." He let them understand who we were and he knew if he didn't say something and we screwed something up in the beginning of the match that things could've gotten ugly. He really helped us out on that one.

The following week, we were going to be at Penn State. We ended up doing two indie shows against Blue Meanie and Stevie Richards before *Raw*; one in New Jersey and one in Pennsylvania on the way to the college. Those guys were hilarious to work with. At the show, we were in the ring and Meanie was doing this spot where he took my arm and started to twist it. Meanie likes to do a lot of funny stuff, and at some point in the match he put Austin Powers fake teeth in his mouth. So as he's twisting my arm, he's trying to look me in the eyes to make sure I see his teeth, and when I look up, we both start cracking up. So then the next day we have another match, and as Rodney and I are driving to Pennsylvania, we stop at a gas station convenience store, where I see the same set of teeth. I bought them on the spot. At the show in Pennsylvania we were doing essentially the same exact match. So when it came time for Meanie to twist my arm, I put the teeth in when he wasn't looking . . . but then he wouldn't turn and look at me. So here I am, standing in the middle of the ring, and I start yelling, "Look at me! Look at me!" He finally turns around and literally busts out laughing. That same weekend, Minnesota had beaten Penn State at football, and *Raw* was from the school's basketball arena, so when we show up to the building, the *Raw* writers tell us: "Go down to the student store and buy as much Minnesota gear as you can find." So we ended up buying maroon sweat pants and sweatshirts with Minnesota on them. We even had baseball hats and Minnesota flags. It was awesome.

Prior to that, we were waiting to go on stage when up walks future NFL linebacker LaVar Arrington. The guy was enormous. I don't know how anyone ever blocked him! And here he is, staring at us all pissed off because Penn State just lost. He was there with Courtney Brown, who went on to be the number one pick in the NFL Draft, and these two huge guys walk up to us, and LaVar just starts shaking his head and goes, "Man, that's cold," pointing at our outfits. We walk out with the flags, and we had so much heat, I couldn't believe it. As we went to the ring, we started getting our asses kicked by Edge and Christian, and as they beat on us the crowd started chanting: "We are . . . Penn State!" The entire arena was chanting in unison. It was really cool.

That show was also memorable, as it was the day of the big race. Backstage of any WWE show is filled with non-stop smack talk, and it's not just the wrestlers; it's the announcers, the agents, everybody. Weeks prior, the Coach, Jonathan Coachman, was talking smack to Tony Chimel, the *SmackDown* ring announcer, and they were calling each other fat and out of shape, so they decided they were going to have a race to settle the score and see who was in the best shape between the two. They had to run one mile, and they picked Penn State for the location of the race since we were already going to be there and they had a track. So, before *Raw*, everybody on the roster went out to the football field to watch the race, and people were placing bets on who they thought would win. I thought for sure Coach was going to win. Coach was much younger and looked like he was in better shape, so I bet $20 on him to win.

So here we all are, the entire WWE roster is in the middle of the football field yelling and screaming over a footrace between two announcers. Rock was there, Austin was there, everyone was talking shit and laughing as Coach ran out to an early lead. He was about 20 yards in front after half a mile, but then all of a sudden it was like Coach's tank went empty. It reminded me of the tortoise and the hare. He had such a big lead for so long that I started to think the race was rigged when Chimel started catching up. Coach was out there talking smack as he ran out to his lead, but sure enough, there was Chimel, slow and steady. And, in the end, Chimel ended up beating Coach. I couldn't believe it. There was so much laughing going on among the roster, it was one of the funniest days I can remember.

A week later was the Survivor Series. I was kind of bummed out because I had really been working hard and I thought the way Survivor Series matches played out, with constant tags and superstars moving in and out of the ring, that I might be able to last a while in the match and prove to the office what I could do on a big pay-per-view. However, it was tough to shine since the Mean Street Posse now had three guys. Three made it rough to work regular tag team matches because one guy always had to sit, and Joey Abs would never sit because he was the most skilled in the ring. It was always between Rodney and me when it came to seeing who would sit out and, most likely, take the fall. So it was always disappointing when I had to sit out. We would all go out there and have our roles, but I wanted to do more, so it definitely got frustrating. I just thought I was better than what I was given credit for, so when I got my chance, I felt as though I had to do whatever it took to prove myself.

At Survivor Series, we were teamed with the British Bulldog, but it was a traditional Survivor Series match, so once one guy lost he was eliminated and the rest of your team wrestled on.

I remember I really wanted to make a great impression, and it was the Posse and Bulldog against Val Venis, Gangrel, Steve Blackmon, and Mark Henry. Bulldog and Val started the match, but Davey Boy quickly tagged me in and I ended up working with Val. (I tagged Bulldog back in but was again in the ring after he landed a vertical suplex on Val.) He was one of my better friends on the roster at that time, so it was great getting to work with him on a pay-per-view like this. He let me get some offense in, told me to hit a belly-to-back suplex and take control, then it was time for him to hit his moves. He told me he wanted to hit a running bulldog so, in my mind, I wanted to jump as high as possible and really spread out to make this move look amazing. I did my best, but was shortly immediately eliminated from the match by Steve Blackmon. My chance to shine came down to taking Val's bulldog with as much air as possible. What's great is, it didn't go unnoticed. The next day at *Raw*, when I got there, Mick Foley pulled me aside and told me what a good job I did taking the bulldog and making it look legit. It's always great to hear from veterans like that because it showed I was starting to improve. It makes you want to do more. So even though it didn't end up being the Survivor Series I wanted, at least when I was in there, I did something memorable. You can't do any more than that.

* * *

On December 13, the day after Armageddon, the McMahon–Helmsley era officially began. Triple H set up a match and the Posse gets our asses kicked by the APA. It was after we had jumped them in the locker room and backstage eight days before on *Sunday Night Heat*. This was the first of many beatings by the hands of the APA, and they didn't hold back as we received some of the stiffest shots we'd ever felt in the ring, including that wicked chair shot I mentioned earlier. But the more matches we did with them, and the more beatings we took, I could feel that we were earning their respect. They were seriously beating the shit out of us in the ring.

The story behind it is that Bradshaw didn't have respect for me when we first started, so he took it out on us in the ring, helping us pay the dues he thought we owed. He would even harass me at home. I remember one time I was in bed with my girlfriend in the middle of the night, and my phone rang. It was Bradshaw. I don't even know how he got my number. It was like a bad dream. He was at the WWE office at Stamford, and I guess he didn't have anything to do, so he called me up and was like, "Pete Gas, you son of a bitch, wake your ass up and come drink with me!"

I'm like, "Bradshaw?" I was still half asleep and really couldn't understand what was happening. I told him I had already been asleep for two hours, and he was like, "I don't care. Come drink with me." I knew then that I had to do it, so I jumped out of bed and spent the last hour that some bar was open with him throwing back shots and drinking beer.

To me, it gave me feeling like I was being accepted. It was one of those things where all of a sudden in the bar, he was acting cool towards me. It was like being back in school and the cool kid might be nice to you in class, but then once he got around his friends outside he always acted like a dick. So now we were in the bar and I was trying to figure out if his friendliness was genuine or if he just needed someone to hang out with. Turned out, he really wanted me to be there and we had a lot of fun. After that night, I felt like I not only had his respect, but that we had become friends. He still could've called at a decent hour, though.

During the McMahon-Helmsley era, the storyline between the Mean Street Posse and Stephanie continued to evolve. There was even one night, during *Raw* on December 20, where they had us dressed in tuxedoes so we could act as her butlers. Looking back on it, it was one of my favorite roles we ever did. It really opened my eyes to something new to the world of wrestling, and that's the comedy aspect. We always played for laughs, but in this specific sketch we had a lot of freedom to ad lib and add things to the script, and every time Triple H would say something, we were standing behind him and I always had a wise-ass remark, and every once in a while he'd turn around and say, "Shut up, you jerk!"

For some reason, him calling us jerks always made me laugh my ass off. We had a lot of interaction with Triple H, and that was great, because not only was he helping us in the ring but we would feed off each other outside of ring and really make it entertaining.

On an episode of *Raw*, the Posse were told by Triple H and Stephanie that we were supposed to face the APA that night. A few segments later it shows us leaving with our rolling bags. Triple H and Stephanie catch up to us and say that if we don't get back in there and wrestle, our asses our fired! As I am walking back in and past Triple H he says, "Ya big bucket head." I always found that to be hysterical.

To me, any time you can bring comedy to the show really helps elevate the entire broadcast. The greatest thing about wrestling is that there's this mix of amazing action, high-intensity stunts, and comedy—and when the comedy is done right, it can really turn out memorable. So, to me, this night as the butler was really my coming-out party.

Ever since I was a kid, I wanted to make people laugh. So as the butlers, it's like the three Mean Street Posse members were playing the role of the Three Stooges. Something would happen, then we'd all point and blame each other. And then Triple H would say, "Listen, I'll give the three of you guys a match against Too Cool." We were like, "Thanks, three versus two, we love it." But then Lilian Garcia announces Too Cool with Rikishi, so again, it was time for us to get our asses kicked. This was the same night when Mick Foley was supposed to fight Santa Claus in a Boiler Room Brawl. He was waiting outside the boiler room when we walked by, and we knock Mick around, hitting him and throwing him into the boiler room. That's when Mick Foley turns toward the camera and says, "Wait . . . did I just get my ass kicked by the Mean Street Posse? That's embarrassing." That was awesome because it made me see wrestling as something more than just fighting. I didn't need to be the tough guy jerk to entertain the fans. I didn't mind making my character goofier. There were already enough tough guys on the roster. Al Snow was doing some amazing comedy back then, and so was Mick. To me, my role was already just to put people over, so the feeling was I might as well make them laugh while I'm doing it.

That same night, with us dressed up at butlers, Al Snow came in to meet with Triple H and Stephanie, and said he wanted to fight the Rock. That was one of the segments produced by Vince Russo. Al was talking to Head and was telling it how he was going to shine it up really nice, turn it sideways, and stick it straight up Rock's candy ass. I was standing in the background and I kept making comments that would make Al laugh, breaking his character, and so they'd have to reshoot the segment. Vince was starting to get pissed because after a few takes, it just kept getting funnier and funnier. Finally, Vince started yelling at us, so we had to stop, but poor Al couldn't quit laughing.

Like I said, my role wasn't to win matches, although I did get one singles victory on national television. What, you don't remember?

When you arrive at the arena for a live broadcast, you bullshit with the guys until around 3 p.m. when they'd put a paper up for everyone to see. It would list all of the matches for the night, as well as who the agent and referee was.

So at that point we'd go see the agent, who at that time was Jack Lanza and Tony Garea, and I'd always make the comment, "Are we going over? Are we going to win the match?" And they'd always respond, "Sorry kid, tonight you're looking at the lights." In other words, I'd be on my back getting pinned staring up at the lights. We won dark matches, but the Mean Street Posse wasn't there to win televised matches.

In fact, my one and only singles victory wasn't even supposed to happen. I was matched up against Thrasher from the Headbangers back in November 2000, who were broken up at the time. Thrasher wasn't in the best wrestling shape during that time and I remember before the match, we were in the gorilla position, and we were going over the final details of the match when, for whatever reason, they tell him he's being sent to Memphis after the show for training. It really fucked with his head. He thought he was too experienced to be sent down to Memphis, and it was definitely a blow to his ego. So what ended up happening is that he gets injured in the middle of the match. Actually, I don't know if he was injured or just quit. So he's lying there and telling me, "I'm hurt!" The referee told me the guys in the back said to end the match. Thrasher was supposed to go over, and normally a guy like him would lead the match. But with him hurt I took control like it was second nature. I told him, "Let me slam you, then I'll go to the top rope and drop a leg on you." Because Thrasher was hurt the match wasn't great but it showed that I was learning how to work on the fly. In the wrestling world, not everything goes as planned and, for once, the lights were actually shining on my back as I made the pin.

Chapter 11

Is That a Wood Chip in Your Leg or Are You Happy to See Me?

This is all leading up to the Royal Rumble on January 23, 2000, one of my absolute favorites to watch as a fan, and now I was getting the chance to participate as a member of the roster.

We had a match earlier that month on *Raw* with the Acolytes where they were making fun of us and said they could beat us with one hand tied behind their backs. So they were still kicking our asses, with just the one hand each, but then Bubba Ray and Devon came down and beat the shit out of them. So they were transitioning the feud from the Acolytes and Mean Street Posse to the Acolytes and Dudley Boyz.

But when we finally got to the Royal Rumble, the three Posse members weren't even official participants, but that doesn't mean we weren't going to cause some chaos. When Faarooq's number was up, all three of us ran down and gave him a beating. But after we ran to the ring, we got tossed out in like 20 seconds.

Later on in the match we did a second random run-in when Bradshaw entered the Rumble. But when we ran in, Joey Abs was like three steps ahead of me and when he dove into the ring he kicked his leg back to the left, which was unfortunate, as he would have nailed me right in the face. So to avoid his foot, I lifted my head up as I attempted to dive into the ring and ended up breaking my nose on the bottom rope as I slid in. So I break my nose and I can't see a thing. Everyone is throwing punches at me and I'm getting hit from all angles. And since I can't react the correct way to move out of the way or block the punches, I'm taking all of these shots for real, so now I'm really getting disoriented in there until Bradshaw finally grabs me and throws me over the top rope. Bradshaw is then eliminated and while heading backstage Faarooq joins him and kicks our ass as we try to leave.

I hustle backstage to try and clean off all the blood. After my shower I go to find the doctor, but Triple H was lying there in pain after his street fight against Mick Foley for the WWE Championship. During the match, Triple H was suplexed and landed hard on a wooden pallet and a piece of the wood went straight into his calf. The wood was about a half-inch in diameter and the wound looked nasty. To make matters worse, every time he moved pieces of the wood broke off and stuck in his calf. There was blood everywhere and he couldn't walk at all and the doctors were working on him backstage, pulling out wood chips from his leg. It was disgusting but, man, Triple H is one tough son of a bitch. You didn't hear him scream. In fact, he barely said a word.

In the WWE, guys would do a lot of things to hurt each other, but never once backstage do you ever hear guys bitch and moan or cry and scream in pain. Triple H just toughed it out as they pulled out those wood chips. I think, as wrestlers, you just build up this tolerance for pain and learn to live with it. Even to this day, if something happens and I pull a muscle or aggravate an injury, I just tough my way through it. A few years ago, I was pitching in a softball game and a ground ball came up the middle. I caught the ball and went to turn the double play, but when I turned toward second base, my hip, which I dislocated back in 1999, popped out of the hip socket as I was rotating. I made the throw, then went down and it hurt like hell, but I continued to play on it. The very next day, I had to go to Manhattan for work, and it was a day where I had to walk ten blocks down to this one building, then ten blocks back to the train. So after that day I decided I need to go to the chiropractor because the pain was really getting to me. When the chiropractor put me up on the table, he pointed something out to me.

"Take a look at your legs." My right leg was a good half inch to an inch longer than my left, and that's because my right socket was out.

He was like, "How the hell are you even walking?"

"To get rid of the pain, I just don't think about it and keep going."

"You just told me you walked twenty blocks and finished a softball game."

"Yeah, don't get me wrong, it hurt. But you just learn to work through it."

He thought I should be in bed, but it's just one of those things; when you're a professional wrestler, pain is just something you learn to live with on a daily basis, and just because my hip popped out didn't mean that I was going to miss playing softball or doing what I needed to do for work.

Chapter 12

My Circus Friends

When I first became a wrestler, my mother used to call it me hanging with my "circus friends." She was nervous as hell even though she'd watched me play football my entire life. But there was something about professional wrestling that she couldn't stomach. She went to almost every football game I ever played in, from junior high through college, and never once got worried. But when she saw steel chairs and tables and everything that was being used in the ring, she decided it wasn't for her. I remember being in a 15-man Battle Royal for the hardcore title at WrestleMania 16. During the match, the hardcore belt could change hands as many times during that 15-minute segment as possible, but whoever ended up with the belt after those 15 minutes left as the champion.

We had been doing this hardcore stuff with Crash Holly for months leading up to WrestleMania. Up to this point we were getting booed for everything, but once the hardcore, 24/7 rule came into effect and we were able to add some comedy to our segments, the fans started to turn and the Mean Street Posse began receiving cheers for the first time thanks to our antics outside the ring and all of the comedy bits we had been doing, from dressing up as clowns to room service waiters.

> For example: We were at a hotel, and we ordered room service as we were beating on Crash, but then we always ended up fighting among ourselves, so Crash grabbed his belt and escaped as Rodney and Abs ran after him. So I said to Tommy, "How about those guys run out after him, but when I run by the tray of food I go back like the fat kid and start eating?" We would do a lot of comedy skits like that.
>
> Another time with Crash happened in Philadelphia. The circus was in town, so we all dressed up as clowns. While setting up the details, I said to Tommy: "How about I use this real high clown voice?" So we have this scuffle, but again, Crash escapes, and when Rodney and Abs come back I stay in character and use my clown voice.

So we get introduced for the Hardcore Battle Royal and the crowd is going nuts cheering us. I turn to Rodney in the ring and go, "Did you hear that cheer? They actually popped for us!" It was amazing. And we knew we were about to deliver something memorable.

A five-year-old Pete Gas at my brother Dan's baseball game.

The 1987 Greenwich High School offensive starters celebrating a victory. We would win the championship a week later. I'm number 75, Shane number 61, and Rod is leaning forward from the back row, number 44.

Me and center Pete Gale of the 1990 UConn football team.

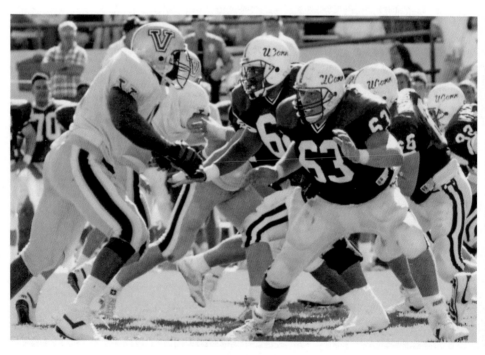

UConn vs. Villanova, October 6, 1990. A game in which we won, 24–22.

Promo shot of Shane and the Mean Street Posse. (Photo courtesy of WWE)

May 1999, Rodney and me in the beginning. (Photo courtesy of of WWE)

The British Bulldog with the "MSP" as his bodyguards, putting the boots to Test. (Photo courtesy of WWE)

SummerSlam 1999, Test ducked out of the way and I hit Shane-O with a street sign. Sorry, Mac. (Photo courtesy of WWE)

Giving a solid leg drop to D-Lo. (Photo courtesy of WWE)

Faarooq and I in the 15 Man Hardcore Battle Royal at WrestleMania 2000. This was just one of the many beatdowns he gave me during my career. (Photo courtesy of WWE)

Promo photo of me in 2000. The MSP went away from khaki pants to jeans and no shirts underneath. (Photo courtesy of WWE)

Tony Garea and I at an appearance in Rhode Island. The man that told me every night that I'd be "Looking at the Lights."

Buddy Wayne's backyard. Our first training facility in Memphis, Tennessee, complete with weight equipment and dead mice everywhere.

My new look for Memphis Championship Wrestling and PowerPro Wrestling.

Rodney, a.k.a. Rodrageous, and me backstage before a show in Arkansas for MCW.

Photo shoot right after a match in Puerto Rico. A towel first would have been nice.

Sightseeing on a rare day off in Puerto Rico.

Paul Bearer and I backstage in Arkansas for MCW. A great man, RIP Percy.

Michael Clarke Duncan and I backstage at WrestleMania 2000 after the show—and after many stitches in my head.

Matt "Prince Albert" Bloom and I grabbing each other's fat at a house show in Knoxville, Tennessee, in 2000.

Having dinner in 2016 with Matt and Scotty. Wrestling friendships never die.

Goldust and I at an appearance. It felt like the more I laughed that day, the worse he had Tourette's.

From left to right. Brian Kendrick, myself, Jeff Hardy, Joey Abs and Shannon Moore in the hotel bar after an appearance down in New Jersey.

Me and Jason "Joey Abs" Ahrndt, with Murray "Bo Dupp" Happer and Nora "Molly Holly" in the background, enjoying a night of karaoke.

Taking a break from an appearance in Rhode Island and sharing some laughs with the Nasty Boys, Brian Knobbs and Jerry Sags.

Joanna and I got married on the beach outside our home on September 20, 2014. As Matt Bloom constantly reminds me, "I out-kicked my coverage" with Joanna.

Jason Fronio, myself, and Rodney enjoying a few laughs at my wedding reception.

On the bus in Dallas heading to the HOF. Terri Runnels snaps a selfie with Joanna and I. Photobomb by Jake "The Snake" Roberts behind Joanna.

Joanna and I before the HOF ceremony. (Photo courtesy of Mike Chioda)

Me and my good friend Shane backstage after the WWE HOF ceremony.

Before the match, when all of us were in the back, everyone talked about what was going to happen once we got to the ring.

"Look, this is WrestleMania. We're going to hit a little harder. Just go out there and fight and when you go backstage after the match, we can hug it out and forgive each other later."

So basically it was on, and we were going to whack each other as hard as we could to make it look great. And as soon as we start, Viscera grabs me and throws me out of the ring. Everyone eventually spills outside the ring and we're using every weapon imaginable. Viscera picks up a box fan, one of those square fans, and that damned thing ended up busting open three or four people in that match. He hit me in the head and I go down, and I start selling it like I'm hurt, but as I'm down I start to feel fluid rolling down my face. At first I thought it was sweat, but then if you watch the video, there is a guy in the front row, and I can still hear his voice to this day as he yells out, "Pete Gas is bleeding!" I look down and I see a puddle the size of a softball on the mat outside the ring, but I'm fine. I could care less about my own blood, so I start pushing and pressuring more blood out of my head. I had an open wound in my hairline and now the blood is flowing really good. So good, in fact, that the other wrestlers are worried. Faarooq comes over to see how I'm doing, the referees come over and ask me if I'm OK, and I keep telling them I'm fine and to punch me in the face. So they're hitting me, throwing me into the poles to help sell my injury.

At one point the whole thing spills backstage and chaos ensues. By now the blood is covering my face and it's in my eyes to the point I can barely see. Rodney wins the title as soon as we get back there but loses it to Joey Abs right away. Thrasher gets on Abs and runs him into the garage door then pins him to take the title. Then Thrasher starts heading back to the ring and I know my segment is coming up so I'm following Thrasher out, and my spot was to pick up a fire extinguisher and spray him in the face, then hit him in the head with the fire extinguisher before pinning him for the 1-2-3. I remember the crowd reaction when I sprayed him, and I remember pinning him and thinking, "Damn, I just won the belt at WrestleMania." Of course, I lost it 30 seconds later, but the fact that I won a belt at WrestleMania, even if it's just for 30 seconds, that's something you can never take away from me. I let out a scream and clenched my fist and I had my crimson mask and, like I said, as soon as I let out my scream, my glory was over as Tazz hit me, punched me a bunch of times, then suplexed me just outside the ring and my reign as Hardcore Champion was over just like that.

It was a big deal because it all happened in front of all the celebrities that were in the front row, like actor Michael Clark Duncan and former MLB star Mo Vaughn.

So we finished the match and go backstage and I head back to the locker room to find my phone blowing up. My brother and friends back home were calling, telling me how great the match was, and then I had like ten messages from my mom and she was crying. Her baby boy was hurt. My mother saw the blood on TV, ran to the bathroom and started throwing up. She said it was one of the hardest things she ever had to watch.

Besides my mom, everyone else in my family—everyone from my hometown—was abuzz about Rodney and me getting a shot. But my brother, Mike, he was my biggest fan ever. He was calling me first thing every morning to find out what was going on. Problem was he would call so early that I didn't even know yet! But he would call and try to find out what we were doing, and any time there was a local event at Madison Square Garden or in New Jersey or Long Island, he would always be there. One of my biggest thrills was one event at the Garden when I knew my brother and some other family members would be there. I was all juiced up as I slid in the ring, knowing they were there. So I go over to the turnbuckle and raise my hands to get the crowd reaction and, when I look down, I see my niece Christy has a sign that says "Pete"; my nephew Michael has a sign that says "Gas"; and then my little nephew Tommy, who was like five at the time, had a sign that said "Tommy Gas" with a sign pointing down. It made me crack up. I always wondered what it would be like to have a child who had that experience of seeing their dad in the ring or to be able to play as them in a video game.

Speaking of video games, I remember when the Mean Street Posse was featured in our first WWE video game: *SmackDown 2* for PlayStation. The Mean Street Posse were hidden characters where you had to win a certain amount of matches before unlocking us, and the first year it came out I went over to my brother's house for Thanksgiving and everyone is in the living room laughing. Apparently my little nephew Tommy was playing a game of "Who could beat up Uncle Pete the worst." He had Undertaker with a steel chair beating the hell out of Uncle Pete. And they weren't even playing against the computer. They had the second controller on the ground just sitting there so my character couldn't fight back as he took chair shot after chair shot. It felt so much like reality because, if I was ever in a match with the Undertaker, that's pretty much what would happen.

It was a thrill, though, because I always looked up to my older brothers. The oldest, Dan, even played professional baseball for the Oneonta Yankees. He was a catcher and held a bunch of records while attending the University of Vermont. He actually played on the same minor league team with John Elway when he signed with the Yankees. Then again, everyone in my family was an athlete. My sister, Patti, was a softball and field hockey star, my next oldest brother, Mike, was an All-American at the University of Connecticut. He was the one who I pretty much compared my life to athletically. He was All-Conference in football during high school, I was All-Conference and All-State. He had two scholarship offers, I had thirty-six offers. So I always compared myself to him and tried to be better, as he was my hero growing up. Well, both my brothers were my heroes, but Mike specifically as we both played football. So to actually have him, years later, come out to my matches and wanting to call me to find out what I was doing was a thrill for me—and any little brother who looked up to his older siblings. There's an eight-year difference between us, so I was really little when I'd go into the locker room after his games.

* * *

One of the toughest things about being in WWE was knowing that my dad never got to see me shine. When I got out of college, my father and I became best friends—closer than we'd ever been. Any sporting event that happened, from the Celtics to the Red Sox, we were watching them together, so I know he would've loved to watch *Raw* and see his son in the middle of the ring (even if I was getting hit with a steel chair). We spent a lot of time together during the week and, on weekends when I'd go out with friends, I knew my dad would be up late so I'd bring home food for us. We'd then sit and talk about whatever happened that night while the rest of the family slept.

Then my dad started complaining that he had been getting heart burn as of late, and I figured it was from eating all these meals in the middle of the night. But the pain and indigestion only got worse, so he had to get himself checked out by a doctor.

The doctor told him he had an ulcer and that they needed to perform surgery. This is September 1992, and by November they open him up and it's worse than just an ulcer: he was filled with cancer, from his esophagus to his stomach.

My dad was a very big guy. He had my broad shoulders and that big, intimidating, old-school look to him. He was a blue collar guy and I can still see him with his jeans and t-shirt and flannel unbuttoned. He was a very imposing figure. I remember taking beatings from him and just thinking, "Don't cry. Don't show weakness." One time he hit me so hard that it made my sister cry.

Now let me be clear: I deserved those beatings, and it made me a tougher guy. Things were different back then, and I didn't hold any grudges over it. And, like I said, as I became older we became even closer.

He definitely mellowed with age and was fun to hang around and talk to. But then we got the news that he had cancer, and it hit us hard. A year prior, my mom's father had passed away from cancer, and my father was the one who took care of him at the end. So when my father found out that now he had cancer, he was really down in the dumps because he had just witnessed what happened with my grandfather and didn't want to go through that himself. But he wanted to fight, so he went to chemo and started all of these treatments. The chemo took the good cells with the bad cells, and it really weakened him, taking him from a strapping 270 to a lanky 170 pounds over the course of three months.

I would visit him each night after work, but he'd be so pooped that he'd barely be able to keep his eyes open. The treatment had him in and out of the hospital on a constant basis.

I remember one time, when he was home, he was sitting on the couch and just spitting up bile. He was really suffering so much, but the thing that really messed with me was that he was always such a tough guy. So when I saw him in those moments of weakness, it was a total mind fuck. I wasn't used to seeing any sign of weakness from him.

He then looked at me after spitting up, and just shook his head and told me, "I just want to die."

It was so hard to hear. Whenever I think times are really tough, I always look back to that moment. Not too long after that, my father called a meeting with me and my two brothers. My sister was in college, so she got spared, but my brothers and I got called to this Friday night meeting. I knew this talk wasn't going to be good. We wouldn't be watching the game.

But I walked into his hospital room and shut the door. I was so nervous, I didn't know what to expect. When I sat down, my father looked at the three of us and just said, "Boys, I'm about to die."

I started crying and didn't stop for a good two and a half hours. He knew time wasn't on his side and wanted to sit down with his boys and talk about life—his life, our lives, our mom, our sister, and his expectations of us as men when he was gone. We all had a part to play in it. Both of my brothers had wives and children, but I was still living at home. I was all about looking for something that was more than just a job, but I didn't know what that career should be. I was lost, but I remember my dad saying that I was going to be the man of the house and needed to protect my mom and not let anyone hurt her. I've always taken that to heart. But for those two and a half hours, it was absolutely draining. I couldn't wait to get the hell out of there. We all hugged and kissed and said our goodbyes, and I was the first one to bust out of the room, but his nurse was waiting for me right outside. This woman was an angel. She took care of my dad through all the tough times and blessed our family so much. And when I left that day, she was there and wrapped her arms around me. I needed a hug, and she had been outside the room crying her eyes out, so when we saw each other we just got it all out together. This was definitely the worst day of my life.

My dad passed away shortly after that. It's sad because you look back on your childhood, and the game would be on and we'd all be watching have a great time, but he'd just puff on one cigarette after another. We'd all pull our shirts over our noses because we hated the smell, but he kept lighting them up. You think about every cigarette that he had and how it destroyed his life, but nobody knew about the risks back then. Everyone smoked. My dad died in March 1993, and I remember thinking how much he missed. He saw so much throughout his life, watching all his kids succeed in different sports, but I just wish he could've seen me at my best. I wish he could've seen me in the ring, living my dream while using his name. He was the original Pete Gas, but I was hoping to take that name to new heights.

Chapter 13

Drama, Dominoes,
and Beat Downs

One thing about the WWE is that there's a never-ending supply of stories and drama. Then again, what else should you expect when you throw scores of athletes together for a non-stop adventure on the road?

In September 1999, we were told to be the British Bulldog's bodyguards. The reason for this, Shane told us, was because Bulldog wasn't drawing enough heat as a heel. So to make him really get heat, they were going to team him with three guys who were already hated by the WWE Universe.

Next thing you know, the Mean Street Posse is out there helping him win matches, and he even won the European title on

SmackDown in October (with our help, of course). So we spent a lot of time with Davey Boy and really got to know him, and what a great guy he was. He initially gives off the impression of being a bit smug and sarcastic and kind of a ball buster, but then when you get to know him you knew better what he meant and he was so easy to get along with. Bulldog used to travel with the Big Bossman, Ray Traylor, and I remember this one time before a match in Madison Square Garden, it was about a half hour before our match, and Bulldog and Ray had put about six Somas in their teeth. It was like they added a third row of teeth in the middle. All of a sudden, the trainer walked by, and they both shut their mouths. But then as soon as he left, they opened them back up to show off their Soma teeth and everyone thought it was hysterical. But when you realize they were Somas, it takes it to a different level.

When I had a bad neck, taking two Somas would knock me out for eight hours, and I'd still feel groggy when I woke up the next day—and I'm 280 pounds. So you had to build up some serious tolerance if you were going to take six Somas a half hour before you were going out to work in the ring. Unfortunately, they had an addiction and needed the pills just to get back to normal. It's pretty scary when you think about it.

* * *

Usually, if there were big disagreements backstage, you didn't settle it with your fists. You went to court: Wrestler's Court.

In baseball, they call it a Kangaroo Court, where guys get fined for things like walking a batter after having him 0-2, and at the end of the year they spend all the money to have a party. In wrestler's court, things are a lot different. In wrestler's court, everything is set-up just like a courtroom. You have a table for the judge, who is usually the guy in the building with the most seniority, and back then it was usually the Undertaker. But on this one occasion he was injured, so the next man up was Triple H. The bailiff was played by the Godfather.

In this case, it was between Teddy Long and the APA.

Sticking with the courtroom scene, the plaintiff, APA, was on the right, and the defendant, Teddy Long, was on the left. So Triple H goes through the whole case, and the entire roster is there. No upper agents or management is allowed to attend. This is strictly for the roster. And everyone is dying to be inside just because it's so funny.

Triple H begins, "This is not like normal court. You can lie, cheat, or steal to win your case. Anything goes and bribes are accepted." The APA brings up the charges, which are that Teddy Long is "a cheap motherfucker." He was being accused of getting free Viagra from a doctor and then turning around and selling the pills to the guys in the locker room (which he's also publicly admitted). He was also accused of always being in the backseat during car rides and never helping pay for tolls. Teddy is the kind of guy who is always digging in his pocket until someone else pays the toll, and he always found ways to drink their beer, eat their food, and never chip in with any money. After all the charges are announced, Triple H looks over at Teddy Long and says, "Teddy, we all know you, so you're pretty much fucked. Do you have any character witnesses that you'd like to bring up?"

"Your honor, I'd like to call my character witness . . . Mae Young." Mae Young waddles up to the front to the table and says, "I don't understand all you wrestlers with your big dicks needing this Niagara."

Niagara? The crowd erupts with laughter. Kurt Angle and I were barely holding each other up because we were laughing so hard. In true Triple H form he looks at Mae with a straight face and starts explaining that sometimes a guys feel they may need this "Niagara." It was easily the funniest moment I had at WWE. Triple H decided in favor of APA, and ordered Teddy to pay up. He was ordered to supply the APA with a 30-pack of beer and a bucket of chicken for two straight weeks after each show.

It was just one of those times where the entire roster was there and were in stitches laughing when Mae Young went up there. Just being there was one of the highlights of my career, especially when I remember all of the superstars from that era who were there; guys who would go on to become legends. It was one of the best times to ever be in the locker room. They only held wrestler's court every once in a while, and any time it happened and I wasn't on the road for whatever reason, I was pissed off I missed it. That was the one and only time I was ever in the courtroom, and it was amazing.

* * *

With so many big personalities, it was a lot of fun hanging out backstage and seeing what would happen next. Some guys like D-Lo Brown and the Rock would play video games while others would play cards or dominoes. Back then, I didn't know how to play dominoes, but I would watch all the guys play and picked up on it pretty quickly and got good enough where I ended up being the Godfather's partner. Undertaker and Kane were always a team. Prince Albert and Rikishi were always a team. And we would play for hours. We would get up in the morning, go to the gym, work out, and be at the arena by noon. And since I was the new guy, I was in charge of holding the dominoes, but I was just thrilled to be part of that group. Still today, I have that set of dominoes the Godfather gave me. We would have a good three hours before they would post the matches for the night, so we'd take over a table after catering cleared and everyone would play. The more you played with someone, the more you got a feel for their playing style, so without saying a word you knew what domino they'd lead with and what the play would be. And the thing about dominoes is, everyone talks smack. You're slamming the tiles down and you're shouting and just having a good time. I remember this one time, it was me and Papa (we all called him that because of his old Papa Shango days) versus Taker and Kane.

Kane is to my right and Taker is to my left, as the game is played clockwise. So every time Kane would put a play down, I would score off him. I was hitting 15, 10, 20, and the more I scored, the more Taker was getting pissed off at Kane. We were blowing them out, and Taker kept saying, "Kane, stop feeding this kid!"

And sure enough, as the game gets close to the end, Kane goes to put down his tile and before he lets go of it to make it official, he turns to me and says, "If you score here, I'm going to beat your ass."

With this, I just look at him with a straight look on my face. I look at him, I look at Papa, and I look at Taker. Then I look at Papa again and smiled. Papa gave his vintage big smile back as I slam my tile down and shout, "Domino motherfucker!"

Kane got up and I ran. I ran throughout the arena, and no matter where I went, there was Kane chasing me. He was going to beat my ass. He chased me up and down the stairs, he chased me through the entire backstage arena, and while I was running my fastest I couldn't shake him. He eventually caught me and gave me a few body shots and one in the shoulder but, luckily for me, by the time he caught me, we were both too tired and laughing too hard for anything to actually happen. I don't know if I've ever run so hard in my life. Taker was laughing his ass off the entire time.

But that wasn't my only physical encounter with another superstar backstage. I remember one night in the summer of 2000 we were in San Antonio, Texas, going over our match before they opened the arena, and while we were doing so, Kurt Angle slid into the ring. But as Kurt slid into the ring, I pushed him out. He was like, "What are you doing?" Kurt and I were pretty close, so I told him, "This is my ring," just fucking around. He went to slide in again, and I pushed him out again.

"I told you, this is my ring." Rikishi was in earshot, and he was always a ball buster, so he starts riling Kurt up to the point where he says, "You know when I get in there, I have to kick your ass."

So I laugh, and I'm like, "You have to get in here first!" At this point, Rikishi starts yelling, "Oh shit, the boy from Greenwich! You're going to let the Mean Street Posse do that to an Olympic Champion?" All he's doing is pissing Kurt off, and Kurt doesn't want to be punked out in front of the entire roster, especially by a guy like me, a guy who can't even wrestle.

Eventually, I just say to him, "Kurt, you want to get in the ring, here . . ." and I go to the opposite end of the ring and lay down on the top ropes like Shawn Michaels used to do. I told him, "Kurt, you can come in now." But by this time a crowd has formed because Rikishi can't stop shooting his mouth off, and when Kurt comes in, he goes, "You know I'm going to kick your ass now, right?"

So we start circling, and I immediately go back to my old football days. I used my offensive lineman moves and any time he was going to shoot on me, I was going to pass block and push him away. I was able to do a pretty good job, moving my feet and shoving him off me for a lot longer than I'm sure anyone expected. And the more I pushed him away, the more of a crowd formed around us. We were having fun with it, but I could see in his eyes that he wanted to get at me. That lasted for maybe a minute, a minute and a half, until finally, out of nowhere, Kurt hits me with a fireman's carry, then sticks his knee in my chest as he starts driving his forearm into my chin as my head is turned. I'm laughing because he got me but, as far as I'm concerned, I won. He was an Olympic Champion and I was able to push him off of me for over a minute. Kurt hit me a few more times, then finally said, "Are we good here?"

So I told him, "I'm not going to break your balls anymore." But then as soon as I stood up, he hit me again with his forearm underneath my chin and knocked me off my feet. He did this like three or four times just to let me know who was king.

And that wasn't the first time things got physical in the ring before they opened the doors to the audience. Back in the spring of 2000, the Mean Street Posse was meeting with Shane and going over a match when Ken Shamrock walks by. Shane is a ball buster, and ever since we were kids, we've always really enjoyed watching as something bad would happen to each other. So when Ken walks by, Shane goes to me, "Hey, don't say that about Kenny!" I start laughing, but then Ken gets in my face and goes, "What did you fucking say about me?"

I'm like, "Ken, you think I'm that fucking stupid?" The night before, Ken and Undertaker had a match, and Ken flipped Taker like a flapjack. So while Ken is in my face, I quickly change the subject, I'm like, "Kenny, how did you get Taker to flip that quick?"

So he says, "C'mon in the ring, I'll show you."

I'm like, "Kenny, don't fucking hurt me. I can't afford to be hurt."

"I'm not going to hurt you. Trust me."

So Ken lays on his back and he has me straddle him, then he tells me, "Punch me in the nose."

I'm like, "Kenny, I'm not going to punch you in the nose." If some freak thing happens and I accidently punched him in the nose, he'd kill me, but he tells me, "You're not even going to come close."

So I'm straddling him and I throw the punch, and as I come straight down, he uses my body weight against me and in the blink of an eye he flips me over completely, just like he did to Taker. He completely reversed the situation and there was nothing I could do about it. He was just that good.

Shamrock is just one of those guys who is a legit badass, and he has an incredible story. One night we were in LA and were driving to Vegas and Kenny didn't have anyone to ride with, so I decided to go with him. We rode together for about three hours, and during this ride he told me about his life and how he grew up living in abandoned cars. He used to live in Vegas where he worked as a bouncer, and told me about how he'd be at home sleeping and he'd get these calls in the middle of the night from guys who were setting up street fights for money. So he'd get these calls, and the guy on the phone would be like, "You have a challenger. The fight pays $2,000." And Kenny would get out of bed, put on some sweats, a pair of old sneakers and a shirt, get to the fight, beat the shit out of the guy in under a minute, collect his money, and go back to bed. I know when I get in a fight, I get a shot of adrenaline so huge that there's no way I can go to sleep. But Kenny is an absolute animal. He's one of the nicest guys you'll ever meet, but he's one of those guys where, if you cross him, you're a dead man. You're dead. He's got this caveman, barbarian quality to him that is just downright amazing. Don't fuck with him. You see movies with these underground fights and you wonder if these things happen for real, but this guy was living it. He had to fight to survive, and that's exactly what he did.

Chapter 14

Meet and Greet

When we were wrestling, we got to meet a lot of celebrities, including some of the biggest athletes of our time. That was really special for me, because growing up in the house that I did, our family was all about teams like the Red Sox and Celtics.

Everything in our family revolved around sports, and my two heroes during my teens were Wade Boggs and Roger Clemens.

So I'm walking down a hallway backstage before a show in Tampa, and just as I look up, I see Wade Boggs is walking toward me. I get all excited because I start thinking of all the stories I've heard of what a great guy he was around Boston and that he was this legendary drinker. But to me, his hitting was second to none. He was hands down the best hitter I had ever seen.

So, as we get close, I decide I'm not going to act all fanboy on him, and I'm just going to say hello and keep walking. But as I get close, Boggs stops, then he points at me and in an excited tone says, "Pete Gas!" What a mind fuck! I just started to laugh, then I told him, "Wade, in 1983 we got cable in the house, and we used to get the Red Sox games on Channel 18, and I watched every one of your at bats your rookie year."

He was so appreciative, and added: "You're not going to believe this, but I almost wore a sweater vest tonight."

We had a huge laugh, then ended up talking for about a half hour about his love for wrestling and my love for the Red Sox. It was such a fun conversation and unbelievable to me that my hero growing up knew who I was when I walked by. He was a great guy and, later that night when I got in the ring, I pointed at him and started acting like I was going to beat him up and we both got a great laugh out of it. It was awesome.

Another time, we were in Houston and I had done a dark match, which is a match before the lights and cameras go on. It's a match to warm up the crowd and get them hyped up before the show goes live. It was also a way the company would train the Posse to work in front of crowds. Since the cameras weren't on, we could go out there and perform a match in front of a live crowd to see their reactions to certain moves or mannerisms.

You're out there in front of a big audience trying to get a reaction out of them. So that night, I really banged up my knee during the dark match and was in the training room getting iced down during the show. All of a sudden, one of the wrestlers walks in and has a baseball with him. The trainer was like, "Where did you get that?" And the wrestler goes, "Roger Clemens is down in catering. He brought his three boys with him and they're all big wrestling fans."

I literally jumped off the trainer's table, ice packs still attached to my knee, and went running down to catering. By the time I had gotten there, the crowd of wrestlers had died out because the show was starting, but then one of his boys sees me and tells his dad, "There's Pete Gas!"

Clemens had brought in a couple boxes of baseballs to autograph, using them as barter to get wrestler autographs for his kids. I had always heard rumors about him—that he wasn't very personable—but for us, it was the complete opposite, especially since he was there with his boys. Since his son knew who I was, he was really, really cool to me, and I still have the signed baseball to this day. He wrote on the ball, "World Series Champs, 99, 00" and I was so pissed because those were the two years he won with the Yankees. I just looked at him when he signed the ball like that, and I was so pissed. I asked him, "Why would you ever leave the Red Sox?" He told me how he didn't get along with the Red Sox GM at the time, Dan Duquette.

And that's what was so cool about all these interactions, as the guys saw you on their level—not necessarily as fans—so they'd open up and talk to you in a different way. They were really getting to know you, and was a position I never thought I'd be in.

Another celeb we got to meet was Arnold Schwarzenegger during a show in Baltimore.

The thing about Baltimore is, the officials take wrestling really serious, and they actually make you get a boxing license in order to perform. I always thought it was cool because now I have a boxing license, and their theory is that if you're competing in a ring, you need a license. One of the strange things you learn while being on the road, I guess. You have to apply for your license, you have to pay a fee (of course), and next thing you know, you're a registered boxer.

So one day, a bunch of us had to go get our license from the city of Baltimore, and while we were there, we look up and Schwarzenegger was standing there. So I went over to say hi, and he was a hell of a nice guy.

One night in Anaheim, we see all of these guys backstage with suits on and earpieces and they were looking everybody up and down as they walked backstage. You'd think the president was there or something, but it ended up being Nicolas Cage. He brought his son to see the event, and I started thinking, *Is he really this paranoid, or did someone threaten him?* Why would you be backstage at a wrestling event and need five security guards surrounding your every move?

Like I said, I saw Arnold just standing there by himself, Wade Boggs walking down a hall, but Nicolas Cage needed armed guards with earpieces? I don't know what happened, but it was the weirdest scene I saw backstage in terms of dealing with a celebrity.

Michael Clark Duncan is another guy who was a huge, huge wrestling fan. Unfortunately, he passed away in 2012, but I have a photo of us together during WrestleMania 2000. It just so happened that during the Battle Royal, I got my head split open pretty bad and I was getting my butt kicked by Farooq right in front of him. Farooq was ramming me into the barrier pretty hard. I was getting stitched up backstage after the match, and then I saw Michael Clark Duncan come walking my way. He asked me if I was OK, and I told him I was, and then he started telling me how he was like a kid in a candy store being backstage at the show. He got all fired up and showed how much he loved the business, so I asked him, "Why aren't you in there with us?" He just said he didn't want to ruin his body, and he was too old to get started now (he was forty-three at the time). Besides, acting paid more.

Within ear shot of our conversation was Mo Vaughn. I'm from Greenwich and Mo was from Norwalk, and we actually had a mutual friend in common who I played football with at UConn. So I went up to Mo and we were talking about our mutual friend for a bit, then he looks at my head, and he can't believe that I was really busted open.

"Those cookie sheets they were hitting you with, those aren't real, are they?" There happened to be one a few feet away, and I go, "Mo, look," and on the cookie sheet that was just in my match, you see blood, hair, dents, and him and his buddy just went absolutely crazy with how bad we had just beaten each other with this stuff. These were big, heavy duty industrial baking pans. Back then it wasn't aluminum, that's for sure. And the trash cans, those gave a little, but not those cookie sheets. Those sheets were legit.

Another fun time was when we were in Los Angeles and Test, Val Venis, Matt Bloom, Rodney, myself, and Joey Abs decide we're going to go to the Mecca, Gold's Gym in Venice Beach. We go there, get a workout, and it's just an amazing facility with all the beautiful people from Hollywood working out there. As we're leaving, Test wanted to go eat and knew of a place around the corner that served all healthy food. So we go over and, while we're eating, Gabrielle Reece walks in. And when she walked in, it's hard to miss her since she's not only stunning, but over 6-feet tall. Test always thought he was a ladies man, so as she got closer he starts bragging about how he's going to score with Gabriella Reece. So when we finally cross paths, she doesn't say shit to Test, then just so happens to say hello to me. It was so funny because here's Test, 6-foot-5, built like a Greek God, and she only talks to me. Test used to call me "Fat ass Pete Gas," so you know him getting the snub hurt his confidence. Matt Bloom and Val always used this moment to break his balls. They'd randomly throw out how Pete Gas has more game than Test, and boy did it hit a nerve. We loved it.

Chapter 15

No "I" in Team

I hear a lot about how people act in the locker room these days. From what I know, the locker room during the Attitude Era was completely different than how it was before and how it is today. Because of the competition from WCW, the locker room was very team-oriented with a focus on winning in the ratings. I remember during *Raw*, Howard Finkel would be backstage watching WCW and comparing notes on what they were doing compared to what we were doing at the same time. Everybody was a team and there was no me-me-me or I-I-I. It was all about winning together. I've been on football and baseball teams, and WWE back then was really like that, where you relied on everybody else to succeed. It wasn't just about who had the craziest stunts. It was about the entire show and making everybody look good.

Every character counted, and every character had that unique twist or look that made them special. There were a lot of younger guys at the time: Edge and Christian, Matt and Jeff Hardy, and there would be guys like Mosh or D-Lo Brown who would pull you aside after a match and give you pointers on what you did right and wrong. They would talk to you about the psychology of matches and why you should do certain things at certain times.

Two of the biggest names who would always help were Road Dogg and X-Pac. They had that match philosophy down to a science, and even though they were two of the bigger names, they still watched the entire show and would talk to you after your match because they wanted to help everyone get better at their craft.

There was one time in Chicago when Road Dogg and X-Pac pulled the Mean Street Posse aside to help learn more about getting babyfaces over with the crowd, while at the same time making yourself look strong. Here we were, new and green, but they took the time to sit with us and help out as much as they could. The most rewarding aspect to me is, twice in the last year, I've actually been able to go back and thank them individually for the amount of time they took with me to learn what came so natural to them throughout the years.

I was recently backstage at a WWE show in Long Island and bumped into Billy Gunn and Road Dogg. Road Dogg now works as an agent backstage for WWE, and I just said thank you, which is something I always wanted to say back then. I hadn't previously gotten the opportunity, as in this business you're on *Raw* one day and the next you're off TV and your days are numbered.

For years I carried it inside that if I ever saw Road Dogg again, I'd pull him aside and just say thank you. So I pulled him aside and I told him, "I owe you big," and he didn't have any idea what I was even talking about.

"You helped me out when you didn't need to, and I really appreciate it."

He gave me a hug and said: "You guys worked hard and always improved and, honestly, you lasted a lot longer than any of us expected." It made me feel really good.

Then, back in June, I did an autograph signing in Rhode Island, and part of the reason I accepted the booking was that I knew X-Pac would be there, and I wanted the opportunity to see him in person again. It's funny, because I saw X-Pac and Scott Hall walk in when my signing session was over. So I walked over to them and said, "Hey, can I get your autograph?"

X-Pac saw me and shouted out, "Brother!" then gave me a huge hug. I thanked him for everything he had done for us, and he became so emotional over the fact that I took time to thank him. He was so grateful, and it was a great moment for me. I'm sure those guys don't get that kind of response from people but, like I said, they didn't have to help—but they did. They saw that this was a team game, and on any team, you're only as good as your worst players, and they wanted to make sure they raised our level in order to help raise the entire team. Since then, I try to do personal appearances and recently wrestled at Citi Field in New York. I'm not only trying to make a few bucks, but make sure I thank my friends, the men and women that helped me along the way.

RKO and Cena

When we first started, we were training at Titan Towers at the studio. They had a ring set up for us and Dr. Tom Pritchard would show us how to bump. From time to time, they would bring out these other young wrestlers to work with us, giving them a tryout to see if they had what it took to make the roster while at the same time giving the green guys some other newbies to work against. There would be a bunch of guys and we'd all mix it up inside the ring. One of the biggest thrills of my career, though, is the fact that at one of these training sessions, Randy Orton's WWE tryout was actually against me. We knew who he was because of his father but didn't really know anything else about him or how huge of a star he'd go on to become.

It's funny, because I went out to WrestleMania when it was in Houston, and I had really good seats for the Hall of Fame, and when Randy Orton saw me, he came up out of the blue, catching me off-guard when he whispered in my ear, "I'll never forget who I had my tryout against. Thank you."

To me, that was such a sign of respect. Here is this guy who is this big-time talent, one of the top guys on the card, one of my favorites to watch, and he never forgot where he got his start. To me, that was the ultimate sign of respect. I loved it.

But that wasn't my only encounter with one of today's stars. We were working out at Venice Beach one day, and working behind the gym counter was John Cena, who was going to school out there for wrestling. It's funny, because we got to know him before he was the Prototype, and one time he even came out from around the counter just to take a picture with the Mean Street Posse. It's pretty funny to think about now. He would always tell us he was training to become a wrestler, how he was going to school, and it's hysterical that he wanted to take a picture with us back then, especially since he went on to become one of the biggest names in wrestling history.

Chapter 16

Rock Solid

I know the Rock is one of the greatest performers in the history of the business but, honestly, he's also one of the greatest guys. Don't believe me? Well, back in the summer of 2000 we were in Oakland, California, and when we showed up to the arena, there were crowds of people lined up around the parking entrance just hoping to catch a glimpse of their favorite superstar. To me, if I could make someone happy by signing an autograph or letting them boo me or whatever, it was worth it and was always fun. But this one specific time in Oakland, I see some fans, so I go over.

I'm signing autographs, taking pictures, and joking around with everyone when I hear a very faint, raspy voice say, "Pete Gas."

I turn around and I see this little boy in a wheelchair. I'm not sure how I even heard him, but I'm so glad that I did because this little boy had tubes everywhere—he had oxygen and wasn't doing too well. I told everyone in the crowd that was near me that I'd be back, and I went over to the kid and treated him like he was my long-lost friend. It broke my heart, but I wanted to do anything and everything I could to help make this kid's day special. I asked him, "Who is your favorite wrestler? Pete Gas, right?" But he shook his head and said, "Rock." I acted surprised to make him laugh. Then I looked up to the dad and asked, "Are you guys looking forward to the show tonight?" And the dad says, "The show was sold out and we couldn't get tickets."

I knew that management always left a few extra tickets for special circumstances, so I told them, "I think you have some tickets reserved in the back. How many did you need?"

"Four including mom and his sister." I told him I'd go check and be right back. So I go backstage and get the tickets and make sure they're in a handicap accessible area, then I go get Rock.

When I find him, I let him know about the fan: "There is a kid outside, and I don't know how much longer he has, but this kid loves you. Would you please bring these tickets out to him and surprise him?"

Like the class act that he is, Rock took the time and brought the tickets and a t-shirt out to him and this kid was beaming. Rock told the kid how he was going to lay the smack down on me, and we put on this act for him, and everyone out there was laughing. But when I looked up over the kid, I see the father, and he had a tear going down his face while he mouthed the words, "Thank you." I would've paid for their tickets with my own money if it came to that.

That moment was so special, and it just made me feel so amazing that I was able to help touch someone's life like that. After that I returned to the crowd and finished signing autographs and taking pictures. While I was signing, another father leaned over to me and whispered, "That was one of the classiest things I've ever seen."

You see John Cena with this astronomical number of Make-A-Wish grants, and I know why he does it. It's a great feeling to touch a life of someone in that way. It's a rush. I always said that if I ever got called back I would want to do even more at hospitals or for sick children. Their faces and the excitement really made me feel like I was helping during a difficult time in their lives. You can't put a price on that.

I'm a nobody, and I know that, but that day I helped make somebody's day special. He got to meet the Rock. He got to go to the show. I have no idea if he's still alive, but one thing's for sure: it's something that his family will never forget. You talk about wrestlers having all this money, all this fame, but something like that? You just can't put a price on that feeling.

And, obviously, Rock is not just a great person outside of the ring, but one of, if not the best performers we've ever seen inside the squared circle. The very first episode of *SmackDown*, we ran into the ring to help Shane and attack the Rock and Mankind. We were hiding under the ring the entire time and couldn't see shit down there. We were trying to figure out what to do, but someone finally signaled to us that it was time, so we rolled out for our attack. Before the match, Rock told me, "Pete, I'm going to give you a Rock Bottom. Throw a punch at my nose and don't make it look like shit. Throw a punch square at my nose. Don't worry, you're not going to hit me. I'm going to hook you and put my left hand on your side. When I give you a squeeze, that's your cue to jump. Then I'm going to sweep your leg and you're going to take a back bump.

He was such a perfectionist and really made you feel comfortable when working with him. He always made sure to go over every big point in each match, and if he knew Rodney and I were involved, he wanted to make sure we were not only able to take every bump, but that we knew how to do them correctly. We always felt really comfortable working with him, and you always knew the crowd was going to pop. He's such a huge star now and deserves it, because nobody works harder than he does. When he was coming up, he was training in Stamford at Titan Tower like I did, so we got to meet before he was the Rock. When we he was just Dwayne, but already had that larger-than-life personality and smile. The reason he's so successful is because he works hard to stand out. He always had his own flair, and it's a tribute to him, because he has such an infectious personality—he makes you want to work hard for him. And in doing so, everyone comes out looking better. Rock is such a perfectionist. No move, no word is wasted, and it's no surprise that he's become such a big-time star.

Chapter 17

That's One Way to Lose Weight

Walking around backstage, it was tough not to have a complex about my body. I was 285 pounds, but all day I was around these guys who were so ripped and look the way they do, and that really makes you feel motivation to get yourself into better shape. So I was trying to diet, and I remember one time when we were in Cleveland and had stopped at a Denny's after a show. Being on my diet, I felt bad for eating all of that junk, so I turn to Rodney and say, "I think I'm going to go throw this up."

Rodney is so competitive. Whether we're in the gym or the ring or wherever, he always wanted to turn everything into a competition. So he says, "You know what, I'll throw up with you."

We go outside to throw up in the bushes, but then Rodney gets the idea to throw up on the hood of our rental car since he had this brilliant plan of wanting to see whose throw up would last longer on the hood as we drove. So, being a couple of jack-asses, we walk up and hurl all over the windshield, and then, just to make sure we did everything as a team, Joey Abs joined in to throw up with us. As we're puking on the car, out comes Matt and Jeff Hardy, Edge and Christian, Val Venis, Test, and Prince Albert. They were all with us earlier inside of Denny's eating, not knowing what they were about to face once they walked outside.

Of course, Jeff sees something disgusting and instantly runs over to get a better look and join in the disgusting fun.

"What are you guys doing?" Jeff asks. So we explain how we didn't want to keep the food down and decided to throw up, but instead of being grossed out by it, Jeff decides to one up us all by sticking his finger in Joey Abs's puke and tasting it. This was so nasty that it caused Christian to run to the bushes and he starts puking his brains out. *Brother Nero, what were you doing?* This goes on for a few minutes before we all hop in the car, and we're laughing so hard because as we're driving, you can see the piles of puke vibrating on the hood of the car. Then, before we knew it, all three piles splattered across the windshield at the same time.

By this time our car is completely covered in throw-up and we're trying to use the windshield wiper, but all that does is push the throw-up to the side and it starts flying everywhere. We're dying laughing the entire drive . . . until we get pulled over by a cop. Rodney rolls the window down, and the cop is like, "What the hell happened to your car?" I roll my window down and I'm like, "Officer, you're not going to believe this, but we're wrestlers and we portray these bad guys, and the fans hate us so much that they actually threw up on our car."

The cop had some mercy and let us go, but I could tell that he knew we were bullshitting him just by the look on his face. Besides, never believe a car full of wrestlers with grins from ear to ear. And that's not even my most disgusting story of life on the road.

There was another time where the Posse was in one car and Test, Prince Albert, and Val Venis were riding in the car next to us. Test took a shit in a paper lunch bag and was trying to light it on fire so he could throw it into our car. But the rib was on them because when Test tried to take a shit into the bag, he missed and shit all over his seat, so Prince Albert was dry heaving in the back, which kind of gave things away that something just wasn't right as they pulled up next to us and waved for us to pull over. They were acting like we had a flat or something, but just by looking at all of them and their expressions we knew they were up to no good.

I looked over just in time to see something being lit in their car, so I just screamed at Rodney to hit it and we rolled up the window and took off. The bag of shit hit the trunk of our car, but we were going fast enough where I avoided getting hit in the face by a flying bag of fire shit. Good times.

But the screwing around wasn't limited to cars, as we fucked around in pretty much any vehicle we rode in. I remember this one time in late 2000, we were flying on a plane headed back to Connecticut. Rodney and I were sitting in the front row of coach, and sitting in first class were Shane and Vince. We were sleeping the flight away when all of a sudden, Rodney gets hit in the face with a rolled up magazine. Of course, it was Shane, because Shane would initiate shit all the time and wanted to make sure we were constantly embarrassed or in pain. So Rodney went to throw it back, but Shane starts ducking behind his big seat while at the same time pointing to his dad, as Vince is asleep in the seat right next to him. So instead of throwing the magazine and potentially smacking Vince by accident, Rodney flips Shane off and tries to go back to sleep . . . but a couple of minutes later, Shane hits Rodney in the face again with a second magazine. Shane starts laughing, and Vince wakes up, and now he realizes what's going on and is pissed that he's now awake, but thinks Shane hitting us is funny at the same time.

We didn't know what to do, but then Rodney signals for the stewardess to come over and has her make the announcement that wrestling superstar Shane McMahon in on board the plane, and he'd be happy to sign autographs and take pictures for all of his fans after he gets off the plane. All you could hear was this big chuckle from Vince. But Shane looks at us and he says, "I'm getting even with you guys." He was so pissed. He probably sat there for like fifteen minutes in the airport signing autographs for people while we all rushed to get our rental car.

Shane's revenge? The following Monday night started a run of the Mean Street Posse versus the Acolytes matches, where they basically beat the hell out of us for at least a month. I can still feel those stiff clotheslines to this day.

These were some seriously fun times for us, though, because as our time in the WWE went on and our relationships with the other wrestlers grew, the boys got to see who we truly were. Along with that came our use of made up words from childhood, as well as other stupid things we did to each other in school.

Our made-up words became so popular, in fact, that we started using them in vignettes. The guys who knew them would pop backstage. They couldn't believe we started to use our backstage vocabulary on air. What's funny is, Edge and Christian still use a bunch of these words to this day. We even spoke to each other on the set of *The Edge and Christian Show* and they said them in almost every episode.

These words are sarcastic and degrading but funny at the same time and a great way to bust each other's balls. Here's a taste of our backstage vocab:

Beater: Easily Christian's favorite word. Beater means jerk off (beat his meat).

Lloyd or Mongy: This word means if someone did something stupid. Like mongoloid. We weren't allowed to say Mongy on the show so we would say Lloyd instead. Honestly, it was a different time back then, and words like this weren't as taboo as they are now. I couldn't imagine something like this ending up on *Raw* today.

Steek: The greatest word of all in my opinion. Comes from the word plastic. Steek has many definitions. It can be an adjective or a verb. It came from our old school days if someone was wearing something imitation or something not brand name. That was steek. A person who is being fake or a phony can also be called steek.

Other childish things we did was play a game backstage called "Mock." You would sneak up on someone, tickle under their chin, and say, "Mock, mock!" This was done by kids in my elementary school. It was called Mock after an old episode of *Happy Days*; the one where Richie, Potsie, and Ralph Malph go to a cabin and make believe they are foreigners. Richie was the only one who spoke a little bit of English and the only words Ralph Malph said were "Mock, mock." So here is an elementary school game that went on to high school and then found its way in the WWE locker room. Shane loved to play it most of all and he was the most creative with it. He would come flying by out of nowhere, no matter where you were, and hit you with a Mock. He did it so much that we all had our hands over our chins when we were hanging out backstage. Later, that move was called "the Mock protector." Shane, Rodney, Edge, Christian, Price Albert, and I would play this constantly. Edge and Shane still play it to this day. I hear at WrestleMania in Dallas, Shane was running around at the hotel and still getting Edge.

Chapter 18

Memphis Blues

There's only so much you can learn about wrestling in a studio with no crowd. So while we were doing a lot of TV and were training with Dr. Tom Pritchard at Titan Tower, we just weren't improving at the rate any of us wanted. You need to understand how to work the fans—the psychology of interacting with the fans—and that's stuff you just can't do in a studio.

So one day in April 2000, we got called into Jim Ross's office and, when we arrived, Bruce Pritchard was also inside sitting by the desk. We had no idea what was in store for us. Were they breaking up the Posse? Were we being let go? Were we about to take part in a new storyline? Sometimes in the wrestling business, you're called to the office and you don't know if you're getting fired or winning a championship.

Our fates were about to change in a way I wasn't expecting as Jim Ross told us that they were sending the three of us to Memphis.

Remember when I first told Shane I wanted to be a wrestler and he warned me about Memphis? That was my first thought. My second thought was *We're going to be off TV?*

But J. R. was like, "No, no, no. Instead of coming home after TV, you're going to go to Memphis Championship Wrestling during the week, then on Saturday mornings we were going to do a show called Power Pro Wrestling, which was a local TV show run by Jerry Lawler. We were OK with anything the office wanted us to do, even if it meant going to Memphis to work shows in front of less than 50 people.

We were told to head down there immediately and find a place to live, and that they would send us down to Memphis the following week. So we had to go home and pack up all our stuff. If we wanted to continue to improve and have a future in the business beyond just being Shane's guys, this was something we had to do. So after WrestleMania, we packed up our cars and moved to Memphis. Joey Abs and I were still single at this point, but Rodney had just gotten married, so Abs and I rented a condo in this gated community and Rodney rented his own in the same community.

But back to our training. You hear about Memphis, you hear about Jerry Lawler, and you'd think the facility would be nice.

Think again.

We used to train in an old ring that was actually from the backyard of former Memphis wrestler Buddy Wayne. No lie, the ring had dead mice on it and weight lifting equipment in the yard that was all rusted and in poor condition. It was a Redneck Gold's Gym, just disgusting

Steven Regal and Jim Neidhart were transferred there to train the group consisting of myself, Joey Abs, Rodney, and Blue Meanie. Regal sees the dead mice on the ring and immediately calls the office. There was no way he was going to let us train there until the entire place was scrubbed down. A few weeks later, we end up at a new training facility in Memphis, dead mice not included. As far as I'm concerned, with all due respect to Dr. Tom, Regal was the best trainer we ever had. We were heels, and he was such a phenomenal heel, such a phenomenal wrestler, that he was able to teach us the psychology of being a heel to the best of his ability. Jim "The Anvil" was great to us but was dealing with his own personal demons at the time. It's a shame I didn't get to learn more from such a legend, and he was someone who I'd admired since I was a little kid. Unfortunately, alcohol was getting the best of him at the time.

The more time we spent with Regal, the better we got, and the more time we spent in Memphis, the more people started flocking to us and wanting to do stuff for us. We had this one stretch of shows where we had to go down to Louisiana then over to Mississippi then onto Alabama, but I had a leased vehicle at the time and was putting too many miles on the car. So this guy comes over and asks me about our shows, and I tell him how far we have to travel. So he goes, "You know what, I have this limo service. Do you want me to drive you guys?" He said he could fit up to eight guys and that all we had to cover was gas. Turns out, it was a Navigator stretch limo.

We get to the first arena and Kevin Kelly pulls up next to us in his Ford Taurus and looks tired as hell from driving so far, and then here we are. We open the door and beer cans are falling out of it and everyone is laughing and joking around and well rested.

So right away, Kevin Kelly asks how we got the limo. I tell him how I met this guy in a bar and he's doing us a favor. Next TV taping we had, we get called to the office.

J. R. and a bunch of guys were in the room and were all very serious. They were like, "You know what you did wrong?" I didn't even know I did anything wrong. They told me, "You know you're in Memphis to learn wrestling and psychology, but you're also there to pay your dues. You know what that means, right?" I understood what they were saying, but Kevin Kelly seemed more pissed off that he wasn't part of the limo.

I like Kevin a lot. He could've hopped in. I literally got called in by five different groups of people for the next two weeks telling me I needed to shape up and start paying my dues, all because of this limo ride. Next thing you know, I'm in the locker room and people want to know why I'm getting called in the office, and Road Dogg and X-Pac overhear what I'm saying.

X-Pac was like, "You got in trouble for what?" Then Road Dogg stands up and says, "Fuck the office. Give me that guy's number because I'm going to use that fucking limo next time I'm in the area." He continued, "Don't worry about what they have to say. Tell Kevin Kelly to suck my dick."

But there was no way around it. Like J. R. said, we were in Memphis to pay our dues. So after we got settled, we went down and we met Terry Golden, who was in charge of Memphis Championship Wrestling. When we first met everyone, they took us to a show at some old west rundown casino. The building was all beat up and dirty. I immediately understood exactly what Shane had been talking about. But the talent in the ring . . . that was another story.

Ron Killings was working down there at the time, and he was just phenomenal. He was the champ and everyone looked up to him. Ron had the moves, the look, the charisma, and was the type of guy who you could use as a role model. He was so good on the mic that it made it easy to study how he handled himself in front of a crowd. I couldn't wait to work with him because not only would he make you better, he would make you *look* better—and that's the key to being a really good wrestler. It's easy to go out there and do a few moves to make yourself look great, but it's a lot harder to make your opponent look good in there, especially if you're a heel. So when we got to Memphis I watched Ron's matches every chance I could. He was also the type of guy who would take the time to help out the less experienced guys like myself. And, lucky for us, they put the tag team belts on Rodney and I the second week we were there. They wanted us to work as a tag team at first so it fit their storyline, but after three weeks they realized that in order for us to get in more work they needed us to work on our own as singles performers.

When you're working as a tag team, you can really hide your deficiencies by standing on the apron and letting your partner handle certain parts of the match. But when you're in a singles match, there's nowhere to hide. You're the one out there in the middle of the ring with the lights shining on you and the crowd mesmerized by your every move. So if you mess up, you can't just make a tag and hide. And that's really the kind of training we needed.

As time went on, we started to develop our own characters, and when they split the Posse up on Memphis TV, it really helped us develop into something more. No longer could we rely on the heat we would get from coming out with Shane or because people remembered the sweater vests. Now we had to work on who we wanted to present to the crowd in Memphis, and I felt like this really helped me improve even faster than I had expected.

All of a sudden, Memphis wasn't this death sentence. It was breathing new life into our careers. We had to come up with our own characters, learn how to be more independent in the ring, master a full set of moves that fit our character, etc.

Ever since I was little, the more I was able to work on something and the more absorbed in that activity that I became, the faster it would click for me. And once it clicked, it's like a weight lifted off your shoulders and everything just slows down for you. When I was playing football, the difficulty increased at every level. It got harder as the guys you played against were bigger and faster, but at the same time you needed to be sure of yourself if you even wanted to be able to compete against them in the first place. And inside the ring, it's the same exact thing. If you doubt yourself, your movements aren't crisp, and it's like you're out there trying not to mess up instead of trying to do something amazing. Once I have the confidence in what I'm doing, I've always been able to take things to the next level. And to me, that's exactly what happened when I started training in Memphis as a singles performer.

* * *

We didn't really have much time to enjoy life while in Memphis. Everything revolved around wrestling . . . except for Thursdays. That was our night off when we didn't have to work a show, so we would train early in the morning to give ourselves the opportunity to go out at night. We used to go to this place in downtown Memphis that was half country bar, half club. Whenever we'd go, we'd bump into Neidhart. One night I even got to be a celebrity judge for the Hawaiian Tropics contest. My job was to sit there, drink beer, and be a judge for all of these beautiful women who were trying to win the crown. It was funny because the announcer asked this one girl who was on stage to describe her ideal man, and she said, "I want a man who is about 6-foot-5, dark hair, dark eyes," and I motion to the DJ, "Is she talking about me?" The DJ stopped everything and was like, "No, Pete Gas, she wants a man who actually wins his matches." We had a good time ribbing each other all night.

Then in August of 2000, four guys showed up from Shawn Michael's wrestling school who really turned the region on its ear. They were Daniel Bryan, Spanky (named for his out-of-ring habit), Lance Cade, and Shooter Schultz. I remember when they first got in the ring, they were all really stiff, though they hit hard. But in talking to Shooter, he said that Shawn would call them once a week when they arrived in Memphis. He kept telling them: work stiff, hit these guys for real, and I don't care how much your opponents bitch and moan. When they bitch and moan, hit them harder, because the harder you hit them and the stiffer your punches and kicks are, the better it looks on television. Shawn told them that you can tell when someone is not working the right way and it makes the match look like shit. So what happens is, when you're in the ring with Daniel Bryan and he's actually kicking you in your knee and laying his forearm into your jaw, which forces you to want to hit him back harder. And to the fans, that makes the match appear more and more impressive. I remember saying to myself, "Man, Spanky and Daniel Bryan are so small." I didn't know how they were going to make it. There's no midget wrestling league. Where are they going to go?

But they became such high flyers, and then Daniel Bryan started to beef up. He was only nineteen years old at the time. He literally came out of high school and went straight to Shawn's wrestling school, and would spend his nights studying the tapes from Japan and trying to incorporate those moves into his repertoire. He was working on all of these different holds and backflips and was really smart about learning when to pull these moves off and how to show them to a US audience who wasn't used to seeing them.

I remember working with Bryan and, man, was he stiff as hell. He really knew how to lay it into you. But it was great because even though these guys were new, they really helped us improve. You really have to tip your hat to that guy, because with his size, he knew he had to be different than everyone else in the US in order to stick out and succeed. Back then he was known as the American Dragon and wore a mask like a Lucha Libre. He was unbelievable when it came to being a technical wrestler, and when you got to wrestle him, you really got into the match because he'd really be hitting you, so you'd really be hitting him back, and it just elevated the believability of the entire match. It looked like a real fight because we were really hitting each other out there, and because you could feel the punch you could really sell it to the audience.

Out of all of the people I saw down in Memphis, I thought Lance Cade had the most potential. He looked like a younger version of Bradshaw and was another guy who really laid it in. He was just a big, dangerous guy who could really do it all. We got to feud for about a month where we literally just beat the shit out of each other. We both understood that we wanted to put on a good match, so like Shawn said, he hit me hard and I hit him back harder and the fans ate it up.

* * *

When we were in that meeting with Jim Ross and Bruce Pritchard, they told us we'd only be in Memphis for three months. Turns out, we were there for an entire year. And the whole time, we kept wondering when we'd get the call to come home. I loved it in Memphis, though. I didn't think I'd like it, but I absolutely loved my time there. It was one of those experiences where you're going through it, and you're like, "This sucks," but then when you look back on it you learn to appreciate the experience.

The most enjoyable part was the television. In March 2001, they thought enough of my skills to put the heavyweight strap on me. I was the champ. I beat Steve Bradley clean in the ring. He had Victoria as his manager, and she kept interfering in my matches throughout the feud, and at one point she reached through the ropes to grab my foot, but instead I reached down, picked her up, and kissed her. The Memphis crowd loves stuff like that. So I not only got to kiss Victoria, I got to beat Steve with the Gas Mask, my finishing move, to win the belt.

My first title defense was the following week against none other than Joey Abs. Steve Bradley came out during the match and all three of us ended up fighting as we went off the air. The week after that, Memphis Pro Wrestling and WWE got into a falling out, and WWE stopped funding the television show. This completely came out of nowhere, and all of a sudden I was stripped of my title. I never lost it, but because WWE broke ties with Jerry Lawler and his organization I was now off the air and had to give up my belt. I finally won the heavyweight championship, but never even got the chance to lose it. Sucks the way everything worked out.

And while I ended up loving my time in Memphis, working down there was a real shocker coming from the *Raw* and WrestleMania crowds. One night I wrestled R-Truth in front of six people. R-Truth came out and there was this woman sitting there yelling at him, and she only had four teeth if that many. R-Truth stopped everything and just started playing his heel role to perfection, talkin smack about the woman's teeth and getting her fired up. But it's like Regal always told us: it's harder to work in front of six people and get them emotionally involved than it is for a larger crowd. If you can have those six people invested in your character and everything you do, you can do it for 20,000 fans. And that's exactly how we learned.

But, of course, we not only learned together, both also had a lot of fun together. Lance Cade actually turned into a great friend and, because of this, I did what all friends like to do: play a rib. During that time I was big into chewing tobacco, so I asked Lance, "Hey, can you grab my can of chewing tobacco out of my bag?" Lance brings it to me, and I'm like, "thanks."

At the time I had my wallet in the car, so I go over to the guy running the show, a guy named Terry Golden, and tell him that I was going to play a rib on Lance and wanted to see how far we could take it. So I go to get dressed then I start bitching and moaning, "Where the fuck is my wallet?" With a straight face I'm like, "We're supposed to be family in this locker room and somebody has the nerve to rip me off. Why didn't you just ask me for money, I would've given it to you! Now I'm missing my credit cards and my driver's license, all because one of you is a creep."

Meanwhile, I go out to my car, grab my wallet, and hide it in Lance's bag while he wasn't paying attention. At the same time, Terry gets a couple of his friends who were cops inside the arena to come over, and they call Lance into a separate room. Poor Lance. He was completely innocent; just this poor nineteen-year-old kid, and now we had him on the hook. I was like, "Lance, I know what you did, just give me my wallet!" Lance denied everything, of course, so I tell him, "Lance, you're full of shit. Somebody saw you put the wallet in your bag."

He started getting really nervous and was sweating pretty bad. Then next thing you know the cops come over and they handcuff him. Lance screams out, "Terry, help! I'm being set up!" I was trying so hard not to laugh and we got him almost to the police car before I said, "Don't be mad, it's just a rib." The poor kid looked like he was about to cry. He was so stressed out. He thought he was going to get arrested and fired from the company. I felt bad because he was so naïve and he was a great kid, but the look on his face when he was being cuffed was just too funny.

But that wasn't my only fun time with the Memphis police. On Friday and Saturday nights, sometimes we would drive down to Arkansas to work a few shows over the weekend. Driving to Arkansas, we always took a specific route, and there was this one stretch of road where I got pulled over almost every time I made the drive . . . and it was always the same cop.

The first time I got pulled over, he says the whole license and registration routine, but I can tell that as he's looking at me, he recognizes me. He grabs my license, looks at my name, then looks back at me and back at my license, and I'm like, "I'm so sorry, officer. It's late and we're just trying to get home after a show."

"Are you Pete Gas?"

"Yes, sir." He tells me to slow things down, then he lets me off with a warning. A few weeks later, I'm flying down the same stretch of road and, next thing I know, lights are flashing behind me. The same cop must've pulled me over at least five times in a two-month period. I don't think I was even going over the speed limit the last two times, I just think by that time he just wanted to say hello. It started to become such a joke that after the second time he pulled me over, he said, "Are you going to drive this fast every time?" But then we'd just laugh and he'd let me go. It's almost like I became friends with a cop by speeding too much. What's funny is, on weekends when Abs drove us in his truck, we never got pulled over. But I guarantee that if it was my truck, the cop would've recognized me and threw on the sirens.

Then again, maybe he was just being friendly, as the overall charm and friendliness was something I had to get used to down in Memphis. When we first got there, it was so much different than New York, especially when it comes to my Northeast attitude toward people. In New York, the feeling is that you cannot trust anyone, and you always felt as though everything was a scam. Strangers don't talk to you in New York unless they're trying to get something out of you.

But here we were in Memphis, and we'd be working out in the gym and random people would just start talking to you or say hi. They would introduce themselves and invite us to barbeques or out to drinks or recommend places to eat. At first I didn't know how to take it. All these people in Memphis were so nice and friendly, but I was thinking to myself, *What's the scam?* I was so cautious of accepting any type of invitation when I first got there, but then I started to realize that it wasn't a scam at all. In Memphis, there really is such a thing as Southern hospitality, and these were the most outgoing, friendliest people I had ever met. I wish it was like that everywhere. I always knew when I was flying back to New York and the plane was full of New Yorkers.

Instead of asking how your day was, all of a sudden people are pushing past you and complaining about everything. There is such a change in attitude when you're going between Memphis and New York. The people in Memphis just made you feel so at home and loved, and it's something I still miss to this day. They make you feel like you belonged, and it had nothing to do with us being wrestlers. The people were just real, down to earth, and friendly.

Chapter 19

Drama

The Mean Street Posse was between storylines and had been told by talent relations that we wouldn't be traveling with the roster until they had something for us. We were instructed for the last five months in Memphis to develop new singles characters. I was in Memphis for a little over a year before the office called and informed me of their decision to send me to Puerto Rico for additional training. I was told by Savio Vega and Dutch Mantel that the WWE wanted me to learn to be more of a "high flyer," because at my size it would be more impressive.

Around the same time WWE bought WCW and, according to the storyline, Shane was going to be in charge of WCW. Dennis Brent from the talent relations department told me that the Mean Street Posse would be going to WCW because it only made sense that Shane's boys be with him when he took over the new/old brand. That's where they planned on bringing us back together with Shane, and then setting up the split down the line so we could make our own paths as singles competitors. That sounded cool, but Puerto Rico? Really? Sure sounded like I was being punished, but everyone assured me this was what was best for me and my career moving forward. So, as I had done the year before, I packed my bags and was off to my next adventure. Goodbye Memphis, hello Puerto Rico!

Once I got settled on the island and found a place to live, I was brought into the main storyline of their IWA show alongside D-Lo Brown and Chaz, and the three of us went in wearing masks and were known as the White Angels. D-Lo and Chaz were also sent down to Puerto Rico at the time because they were told they needed to develop their characters and hone their skills, both inside the ring and on the mic.

IWA eventually had us rip off our masks, and when people saw who we were, we were babyfaces right away because of all the TV exposure we had gotten while in the WWE. Everyone knew who we were, and the crowd went insane when we ripped off our masks. Wrestling was (and still is) a really big deal in Puerto Rico, and on the island they seriously believe this stuff is real; so real that when we walked around the island, people were actually afraid of us like we were going to piledrive them into a t-shirt stand or something. You would actually have people walking your way and cross the street once they realized a professional wrestler was walking toward them. It was unreal.

When we were working in Puerto Rico, we used to wake up, go to the gym, come back, and then go do some cardio before putting on our bathing suits and walking the beach. This was pretty much our daily routine. I remember this one afternoon when I was walking with a friend of mine on the beach, and we were going to meet his girlfriend. As we're getting closer to her, I notice that there were these three guys with a camcorder, and it looked like they were trying to film her in her bikini. She told us she was starting to feel uncomfortable, and when we looked back at the guys again they had their camera aimed right at her crotch. The three guys were all in their early twenties, and when they saw us looking at them they started acting like tough guys and yelling at us like we were the ones doing something wrong. So I walked up to the guys, snatched the camera, and basically told them in Spanish that I was going to throw their camera in the water. All three guys looked ready to fight, so I squared up and was ready to take on all three of them if that's what it took. But then they started speaking to each other in Spanish and were talking too fast for me to understand it, but then I hear one of them say, "Pete Gas!" and the other two were taken back by it and actually let loose with an audible gasp.

So there we are, about to fight, and then as soon as they realized who I was, their tone changed and they were very apologetic. So I gave them their camera back but did the Dikembe Mutumbo finger wave and told them not to film the woman again. Imagine what would've happened if they saw Kane or the Big Show walking on the beach. They would've shit their pants. We went on our way, but my friends were actually upset that I stood up to those three clowns because there was so much crime in Puerto Rico at the time and so many people getting killed over stupid shit that they didn't want me to end up dead over a videotape. You never know who these guys could've been or if they were strapped. I wanted to stand up to them but, looking back, it probably wasn't the smartest thing I ever did. At the time, however, I felt as though I needed to take a stand, even if it meant throwing down against three guys.

In the States? Different story as we have fans, but 99.99 percent of them understand that what we're doing is scripted out for entertainment. We lived in Memphis for a little over a year and they loved wrestlers, but there were definitely times when people wanted to fight us to see just how tough we were. Then again, we were never looking to get into a fight because we knew the company was watching your every move, and the last thing the company would want was bad publicity.

In Memphis, we'd go to this nightclub Denim and Diamonds, and you'd always run into some idiot who would say something like, "You're supposed to be hardcore? How about I hit you over the head with a bottle?" They're excited that a wrestler is in the bar and they want to step up and show how tough they are. They think they can handle us but, truth be told, the wrestling moves we learn, if we did them for real, we could really hurt somebody. So even though we're not hurting each other in the ring, you know if you did some of these moves for real we could really fuck somebody up. That means you always have that in your back pocket if something goes down, but at the same time you know nothing is going to stop a gun or a knife or a beer bottle to the back of the head, so you just try to defuse any confrontation as quickly as possible. Even though you know you can beat a guy's ass, you don't want that phone call from Vince because that could be the end of your career.

And I know that for a fact. When I first got to the WWE, I was driving a Jeep Wrangler. After the first six months of being on the road, I treated myself to a new Jeep Grand Cherokee. So I'm driving down the road and am behind this lady, and she was either going too slow or stuck at a light, and I beep the horn. She hears the horn and starts flipping me off, and I gave her the finger, and then she starts flipping out and cursing and screaming and yelling at me. She must have had a really bad day, but she was going off on me, and then I notice she has a kid in the back seat, so I take off and continue on my day.

I'm driving from the WWE offices to the Stamford Mall, and I go do my shopping, and next thing I know I get a call from Shane. He asks: "Where are you?" So I tell him I'm at the mall, and then he tells me that the cops are surrounding Titan Tower looking for me. I was like, "Why?" And I can hear Vince in the background, and Vince is pissed off beyond belief.

"Did you have a confrontation with a woman? Did you tell her you were going to beat up her and her child?"

"What?!" Apparently she had taken down my plate number and called the police and told them I threatened her. All I did was beep the horn. It was all of two seconds of my life and I just went about my day, meanwhile the cops were out looking for me thinking I had threatened this woman.

So Vince says, "If he thinks he's so tough, let's see how tough he is when he gets into the ring next week." I was like, "Shane, I've never lied to you. I've never lied to your father. The most I did was flip this lady off. Somebody must've pissed in this lady's Cornflakes or something, but I guarantee you she can't even pick me out of a lineup. She has no idea what she's talking about.

All being said, everything got squashed and she eventually told the cops the truth about what happened. Vince later pulled me aside and told me that this was a valuable lesson for me to learn.

"This is why you have to keep a cool head, because it's not Pete Gasparino, it's Pete Gas from the WWF who threatened to beat up a kid." I never wanted to give Vince the option to fire me for a reason like that, so I just never let anybody get to me. But I'm lucky this happened back then and not during the age of Twitter, or I would've been all over *TMZ*.

Chapter 20

Island Life

I had been in Puerto Rico for about three months and was really learning a lot and gaining confidence as a performer. I always wondered why they sent me to Puerto Rico, as I was the only one from Memphis being sent, but Chaz and D-Lo always told me that it was because the office saw something special in me. I always wondered if the office was trying to tell me something, like they wanted to prove a point by sending me out of the country so that I could continue to pay my dues.

Back in the Attitude Era, there were five or six writers behind the scenes who each wrote for a specific character. We had a guy named Tommy Blancha, and Tommy was fantastic. We had more fun doing the hardcore 24/7 matches than anything in our careers, as Tommy included us in all of the storylines and ideas. We would go to the location, then we would have some say in what was going to happen.

I really enjoyed the creative freedom Tommy gave us to just have fun and add some comedy to our segments. Tommy ended up leaving the WWE to go work on a sitcom, and when he left, Brian Gerwitz started picking up some of the writing. While Brian and the other writers kept us on for a while, you could just tell that every week they had us do a little less. Tommy was our main supporter. So when he left, we were slowly being written off the show. They just didn't know what to do with us anymore. With Tommy, we'd be leaving the arena at the end of the night and he'd be in the corner by himself giggling and call us over to pitch ideas for things we could do. We would sit there with him and laugh and talk about different ideas. But once he left, it just wasn't the same. We were no longer given the opportunity to add our own ideas, and when we did they ended up being used for somebody else. But more about that later.

* * *

Everyone kept telling me I was really improving, but at the same time I always felt like there were certain people who would never like us because of the route we took; because we were Shane's friends. Were they actually trying to help me, or were they killing my career?

D-Lo and Chaz kept telling me it was all for the good of our career, but in the back of my mind—especially when I first got there—I felt as though I was being punished. But in the end it didn't matter, because I could see that I was really hitting my stride as a performer, and if the WWE office heard how good I was doing, I felt like I would get a fair shot when I got back to the States. All I needed was the chance to prove I wasn't the same green guy they saw in the sweater vest.

The other great thing about being in Puerto Rico was seeing the fan response to what we did in the ring. Like I mentioned before, the locals really thought wrestling was real. If you were a babyface, you were loved, but if you were a heel, they would go to extremes to show how much they hated you. Fans would throw cups of piss at you, they would pick up pennies, hold them with pliers, then heat them up with a lighter. Then, when you walked by, they would throw them at you. And if you weren't wearing a shirt, they would not only burn but stick to you. It was nasty.

There were only two buildings on the whole island where we wrestled that had air conditioning, and I remember driving to the arena and seeing all of these little kids lined up outside. It reminded me of a *Little Rascals* skit because they had a horse with a big dip in its back and kids were riding these horses to the matches. But all these kids were lined up down the street, and they all had these bags and were picking up rocks and filling their bags. I remember asking some of the guys, "What the hell is going on with all these rocks?" And they told me, "These kids sell bags of rocks to fans for a dime. That's how they make money before watching the show."

So these kids sell rocks to fans, and then the fans would actually throwing them at us as we walked toward the ring (along with dumping cups of urine on us!). It was pretty fucked up. I was fortunate enough to be a babyface almost my entire time here, but even as a face you had to watch out because it's not like these fans had great aim. We'd be in the ring and you'd have someone in a headlock, and next thing you know your ears are ringing because you just got smacked in the head with a rock. I'd rather get hit with a rock than a cup of piss. It was just vulgar.

* * *

Our trainer down in Puerto Rico was Savio Vega. I had been blessed with a lot of great trainers from Dr. Tom Pritchard to William Regal to Tracey Smothers to Jim "The Anvil" Neidhart to Bobby Eaton, and everyone brought their own unique style and flair to training and what they taught us. By the time we got to Puerto Rico, they were trying to make me into a high flyer, which I thought was pretty cool.

I remember one time when they gave us directions to where we were going to train that day, and we're driving and we're looking for a gym. Instead, we pull up and there were four pillars with a tin roof. It was cooler to be outside. I would've rather been outside training because as the sun hit the tin roof, it made the ring inside hot as hell. It would've been better to wrestle on concrete.

Savio brought in myself, D-Lo, Chaz, and a bunch of guys who were trying to make it in development. Savio saw me doing a dropkick and he liked it, but he wanted to see how high I could get with this dropkick. So he went and got this 7-foot-tall guy, had us stand toe-to-toe, and told me to dropkick him. I start to step back, and Savio waves me off. "No, no, no, no, no!" he says as he pushed me closer to him. "Now dropkick him in the chest."

At 7 feet, that's pretty high. I had to get my feet up at least 5 ½ feet, but I just looked at the guy and did it. When I kicked him in the chest, Savio was so happy that he actually popped.

I did it on the first try, and I really felt like I was starting to get better to the point where I could finally compete on the WWE level.

I was so happy with the way I was progressing, especially since I was able to work with D-Lo and Chaz. They really boosted my confidence, because Rodney and I were so green when we came up, and when you're only working with another green guy it's hard to take that next step forward and advance. When you're both green, you don't know whether or not you're doing something right or wrong. But when you're doing something out there every day with seasoned veterans, that's when you really learn. I just felt like I was picking up the little things that made all the difference. In wrestling, you're always learning something, whether it's moves or psychology or getting over with the crowd, or even working on the pitch of your voice so you come across better to the crowd, and learning from those guys was just so valuable.

In the upcoming weeks, my character (as well as Chaz's) began to change. While D-Lo continued to be a babyface, they made us heels. Being a heel was something I was familiar with and it came naturally. Chaz and I were a tag team and were able to get some good heat with the crowd. In addition to working tag matches, we would do singles matches as well. One night I had to work a match with a wrestler named Glamour Boy Shane. He had long blond hair and his gimmick reminded me a lot of Shawn Michaels. He was beloved on the island and with my recent heel turn, it made for great heat with the crowd. The fans on the island really loved when the wrestlers actually took the fight into the stands. I remember thinking I was going to get stabbed or something. I did end up bloody . . . but I did it to myself.

After quickly leaving the ring we end up in the crowd and were really laying shots into each other. I had the upper hand on Shane when he blocked a punch and decided to ram my head into the concrete steps. I knew I had to make it look good but I got too close to the steps and split my head wide open (obviously I made it too good). When I lifted my head I saw the crowd around me had scared looks on their faces. That's when I felt the blood pouring down my face. We continued to fight outside the ring and I was bleeding so much there were puddles all over the gym floor.

The referee was really concerned and wanted to stop the match. He didn't understand English and I was trying to tell him I was fine while staying in character. Eventually he stopped the match and the crowd was livid. They were booing and throwing things at me and I was playing it up and challenging them to fight. When I got backstage I explained to Savio and Dutch that I was fine. Savio sent me to the showers but my head wouldn't stop bleeding. He told me to go to the hospital and get stitches.

On the way home, I told Chaz and D-Lo a story about Joey Abs. Back in Memphis, Abs went to slam Jack Dupp and his loop earring caught Jack's belt buckle. It ripped his earlobe to the point that it was hanging. We ended up using Crazy Glue to close the wound. And not the one used for cuts—that didn't exist yet. We used real Crazy Glue and put his earlobe back together like it was the handle to a coffee mug—and it worked!

Back then the hospitals in Puerto Rico were so packed that I would have sat in the ER for hours, as my injury wouldn't have been seen as a priority. In fact, I probably would have been there all night before being seen. I asked D-Lo to stop at a store and I bought the glue. We went back to my place so I could shower and then Dr. D-Lo and Dr. Chaz went to work on my head.

The bleeding stopped instantly, but with one small problem: because the cut was on the top of my head, my hair around it had hardened. Every time I hit it washing my hair in the shower I saw stars. Just one of the many laughs we had on the island.

Another night we decided to make a bet about who could buy the most Somas from one of the Puerto Rican pharmacies without them kicking us out. Somas were really big in wrestling life back then, especially when it came to dealing with painful injuries. It wasn't even a dollar a pill, which still seems ridiculous to me. So D-Lo walks up the pharmacist and goes, "I'll have 20 Somas please," and the woman behind the counter just hands him the pills. So Chaz is next, and he wanted to outdo D-Lo, so he's laughing and goes, "Can I get 100?" No problem, the lady hands him 100 pills. I'm next, so I'm joking and I go, "Hey, can I get 500?" The lady was like, "Sure." I couldn't believe it. I didn't even want them, but here she was willing to sell me 500 pills. We were all laughing so hard, but it shows how easy it is to get your hands on these drugs when you're outside the United States.

Chapter 21

Nightmare on Mean Street

I was down in Puerto Rico a little over three months when, seemingly out of nowhere, the day every wrestler dreads happened.

It was a Wednesday, and I was with Chaz and D-Lo. It was about an hour prior to us leaving for a show and I get a phone call: It was Joey Abs.

"Hey man, I got to talk to you. I need someone to pick my spirits up."

"What's wrong? Is everyone OK at home?"

"I just got released."

I couldn't believe it. He told me Bob Clarke was down in Memphis and calling guys into an office one by one, and you were either leaving to train in Louisville or were getting your head chopped off. I asked him who had survived thus far, and he told me Lance Cade and Spanky and Dragon (a.k.a. Daniel Bryan) were heading to Louisville. Back then, Brock Lesnar, Randy Orton, and Batista were in Louisville. That's where a lot of the big guys now were training back then, but it was cut day and not everybody was surviving.

The WWE had decided to do away with their Memphis affiliate. Something had happened between the office and Jerry Lawler, and Memphis was Jerry's deal, so everybody went their separate ways.

Next thing I know, Rodney gets on the phone and tells me he's been released as well. "You're lucky you're not here, they're letting everybody go." I tell him sorry, and I don't even know what to say, but now *I'm* getting nervous. Yes, I'm in Puerto Rico, not Memphis, but they just released two-thirds of the Posse and I knew I could be next.

Later that night, I'm pretty somber in the back of the car and Chaz asks me, "What's the matter?" So I tell him I have a bad feeling that I'm going to get cut. Then D-Lo turns to me and says, "You're not in Memphis. You're in Puerto Rico, remember that. They sent you here for a reason. They already broke you guys up. You're not the Mean Street Posse, you're Pete Gas." So that made me feel better, and we went on to go do our show.

When we got back, I decided to walk a mile down to the grocery store and picked up easily $100 in groceries for the week. I'm carrying them all back to the apartment as part of a workout and sweating like a pig, when next thing I know my phone rings. It's Bob Clarke. I see his number come up and I'm like "son of a bitch." I answer the phone and Bob asks me if he caught me at a bad time. I tell him how I'm walking back from the grocery store and he stutters, "Oh, oh, I'll call you back." I was like, "Just give me the fucking news!"

He goes, "Well, the office is making some changes and we have all these guys from WCW now that we bought them and the Monday Night Wars are over, and we have too many guys and not enough airtime, so we're cutting some guys and we've decided to let you go." He told me he was going to get me in contact with "Dr. Death" Steve Williams and some guys in Japan who were looking for wrestlers, and that the plan was for me to go to Japan. And when I had improved to their liking, they would bring me back. "We know you've been working hard, we know you dropped 40 pounds and look great, and the office can't believe how good you're wrestling."

I was completely devastated. If they thought I was working hard and wrestling great, why the hell was I being cut? Later that night I get a phone call from Shane.

"Pete, I'm sorry. It was a business decision." He told me he didn't know it was going to happen. Years later, however, he told me that he did actually know beforehand. Rodney wouldn't even take Shane's calls for a while, he was that upset. And it's sad because Rodney and Shane grew apart because of this and their friendship has never been the same, even to this day. They were friends years before I even came into the picture, and the strain this caused on their friendship hurt them both personally.

As for me, it only took a few days to write me off of Puerto Rican TV, and I was off the island for good.

Chapter 22

The Comeback

After I got released, I wasn't ready to quit the business. I got a great phone call from Chris Benoit, which I was shocked about.

"Pete, sorry to hear you got released. I followed you since I got to the WWE and I watched you every week, and you're not bad . . . you're actually pretty good. Don't quit. Don't quit the business. Keep doing stuff, keep working out because you never know if you'll be called back."

I'll always remember and appreciate that phone call because when you have guys with that much talent reach out to you, it makes you feel pretty special.

After I get released, I see Brian Gerwitz one day in the Stamford Town Center. He was at the food court with a couple of other writers, and I go up to him to pitch an idea I had been working on for my character. Remember when I mentioned stealing our ideas and using them for somebody else? Well here goes: Obviously, being from the Mean Street Posse, my character had money, and my idea was that I was going to start losing all my money through a gambling addiction. The APA was going to start taking my bets on other sports then, all of a sudden, I'd start betting on wrestling. I had an entire angle with this that could've lasted over a year, as the deeper I got in a hole I'd start doing run-ins to influence the match and change the outcome. I'd be doing anything in my power to win my bet, and this would lead to other feuds because I'm screwing over friends by interfering in their matches.

Eventually, the APA would tell me that if I throw my upcoming match, they'll clear the books and I won't owe them anything. But when I leave the APA, I run into Stephanie and she says, "From my understanding, there's been a lot of gambling going on around here and rumor has it you're a heavy favorite in your next match. Just know, if you lose this match on purpose, you're out of the WWE." I thought with this storyline, people would be invested in my character and they'd want to see if I fix the match and lose my job, or get in even deeper with the APA. The writers loved the idea.

In fact, they loved the idea so much, they decided to make a gambling storyline with the F.B.I. (Full Blooded Italians). I'm pitching my idea to them on how to bring me back, and they took my idea and did a shitty job with it after giving it to someone else. I don't think the storyline even lasted a month before they dropped it. They just didn't know how to run with it. The thing is, I'm pitching the idea to Brian, and he's loving it, and he's telling me how realistic the angle is and how many different ways the angle could go, then he uses it for somebody else. It just made me sick to my stomach, especially since we already focus tested the gimmick while we were down in Memphis fooling around, and I'm sure it would've worked.

Imagine if, when *Monday Night Raw* started, I tell everyone I have $50k riding on the Bills in *Monday Night Football*. People could be following along to the score of the game during our broadcast. I think it could've been huge. That might have been my opportunity to come back.

This is the way we did it in Memphis:

Rodney and I had a tag match and, when I came out, I brought out a television set. There was a college football game and I had a bet on Florida State that night. (The game was actually on the television.)

Kevin Kelly came down and he would give me updates on the game during the match. So while Rodney was wrestling, I'd leave from time to time to go watch the game and check the score. From time to time Kelly would yell "Fumble!" and I'd turn my back and Rodney would get jumped. Rodney ended up getting beat and it caused a huge rift between Rodney and me, and that's what split us up.

Instead, I went back to sitting at a desk and working a "regular" job. I'd so much rather be a jobber than work a job any day of the week. Man, was it tough to go from WrestleMania to an office job, but we didn't make enough money wrestling to just retire and wait for Shane to maybe call us back into the ring. All my friends, all the people I met, they all assumed I had Shane's level of money because we were on TV, and that the stories of the Posse vignettes were now somewhat true, thinking I had been paid millions while with the WWE. They thought I'd be driving a Bentley for life or something because they saw me on TV. And while nobody really tried to take advantage of me, people look at you strange when they recognize you from TV and you're not driving a luxury car. When they saw I was still driving a Jeep, they couldn't believe it, but it was a big deal to me. To be honest, when I upgraded from a Wrangler to a Cherokee, I thought that was the greatest thing ever, no matter what other people thought. No matter how big I ever got or how much money I made, I always just stuck with Jeep. I guess that's just who I am.

But the superstar image people projected on me went beyond cars. When I came back home, I'd go to a softball game and if I didn't go around and shake everyone's hand, especially down in Greenwich, you got looked at very differently. I remember one guy, I went up to him during a game and he was like, "Oh, I wondered if you were now too good to say hello." I remember thinking to myself, *Why would I be too good?* I never changed who I was. I never thought I was better than anyone else. But when people see you on television they see you differently, when in reality you just have a different job. I tried to stay close with people and to always be very humble. I knew where my bread was buttered and was always very appreciative for what I had. There's an old saying: remember the people you see on your way up because you're going to see them again on your way back down. And from what I saw, there's no saying more true.

I have to admit that my life was really hard after wrestling. I struggled for sure. Post Posse, I went and worked on Wall Street as a bond broker, and you can't leave the desk because you never know when a trade is going to come through that you need to broker. So you're constantly by the phone waiting for it to ring or for someone to yell out so you could quickly get on the phone and broker a deal to someone if they're willing to buy the bonds. You're literally trapped in a chair for at least eight straight hours. I'd be there from 7 to 4, and felt like a caged animal. There was no freedom and every day felt like the same, where in wrestling every day was different. You go from being a star and people wanting to buy you drinks or dinner to going out on a Thursday night trying to solicit business, and now you're buying clients dinner hoping that they'll do more business with you. It's two completely different worlds.

After 9/11, the broker business tanked. Money wasn't going anywhere as people were becoming more frugal with their savings, so that was the end of that job.

Total Nonstop Posse

Even though I was now on Wall Street, I still had the itch to get back into the business. Out of nowhere, Jeff Jarrett called me up and told me he was starting up a wrestling company, which turned out to be TNA. We got to talking, and I always had a lot of respect for Jeff. I remember when he was getting ready to leave WWE for WCW and I actually went and looked for him backstage so I could say goodbye. He was such a great guy, so to me not only were we losing a valuable member of the roster, but beyond that I was losing a friend. I always held him in high regard, so when he called me up about TNA I was all ears. We got to talking about the possibility of me joining the roster, and I told him how I didn't want to quit wrestling, how I had it in my blood, but after WWE bought WCW, there really weren't any alternatives for those who the WWE eventually let go. I was hoping TNA could be the alternative everyone was looking for. He told me, "Pete, if we take you on, you're going to have to bash the McMahons and WWE." I remember feeling sick to my stomach. I was like, "Why can't I just be Gas or some other name close to who I was in the WWE? Why did I have to go in and bash the McMahons?" But he was insistent that if I came in, that's what I had to do. He asked me, "Do you feel comfortable with that?" And I said, "No, but I want to talk to Shane first." Obviously, Shane being one of my best friends, the last thing I want to do is insult him or his family, even if it was just a character being played on television. It just hit so close to home, too close to home for me, and after much thought I just realized that it wasn't something I wanted to do to someone who I cared so much about. So wrestling in TNA was out, and I was back to working my desk as a bond broker the next day, despite how much the ring continued to call my name. As much as I still wanted to be in the business, there was something about being loyal to the McMahon family that just meant so much more.

With my current gig, I'm with WB Mason. I live on Long Island, but I work back in Greenwich, so the drive is a good seventy to ninety minutes depending on traffic. People ask me all the time if I'm sick of driving, telling me the commute must kill me, but it's nothing compared to what I used to drive. I wake up now at 4 a.m. and go to sleep at 8 p.m., which is the complete opposite of the WWE lifestyle. We wouldn't even pull into the hotel until 3 a.m. after doing a live Raw, and you're sleeping until 10 a.m. before going out and heading off to the arena. So driving never bothered me. In fact, it's my down time, so I enjoy it. I just wish I had my wrestling partners back with me for my commute. We told so many stories—now that's the way to really kill time on the road!

Then again, if I was still with the Posse, no way I would've met my amazing wife, Joanna. We met in May 2012, and the best thing was that she had no idea who I was. When we met, we were talking and I mentioned to her that I used to wrestle for the WWE. She wasn't a fan and had no clue. She watched a little bit back in the late '80s when her brothers had it on television, but the extent of her knowledge was Hulk Hogan. She ended up calling her best friend, Lisa, who is this huge wrestling fan. "Do you know some guy named Pete Gas?" Her friend then gave her the whole history of my character; how I wore a sweater vest and won the hardcore title twice. She broke down my entire career, it was too funny.

Now there are days when I have a softball game and *Monday Night Raw* will be on, and my wife will have wrestling on television. She's hooked. She's totally addicted. In December 2012, WWE was working at the Nassau Coliseum, so I called Matt Bloom and we made plans before the show to meet up at the parking ramp. Matt ended up bringing us backstage and Lisa's jaw dropping because she got to meet the New Age Outlaws and Tensai. She couldn't believe it.

My wife's favorite wrestler is Kane. So as we were walking down the hall she sees Kane and he had his full gimmick on, complete with menacing mask, but he came right over and gave me a hug. He shook my wife's hand, and she was expecting this deep, dark voice, but instead he was like, "Hey, my name is

Glenn, nice to meet you," in just his regular, Glenn voice. She still jokes about it. At the end of the night, the house show had a cage match between John Cena and Dolph Ziggler. And after Cena won, for some reason our eyes met, and he goes, "Hey, Gas!" I was cracking up. So Cena climbs to the top of the cage and throws his armband down and motions for me to give it to my wife. She wanted nothing to do with the sweaty arm band, so I gave it to a little girl that was near us. But when I did it, Lisa was pissed like, "Why didn't you give that to me?" It was too funny.

My wife's an attorney and she'll be in court and other lawyers will come up to her and ask, "Is your husband Pete Gas?" She gets a kick out of how many lawyers will see us sitting ringside at the Nassau Coliseum and want to know more about the wrestling world. It's also crazy for her to see me back in my element, where fans are actually approaching me for pictures and autographs. Still to this day, the fans seem to get a kick out of the Mean Street Posse. And believe me, I still get a kick out of the fans.

Chapter 23

Friends 'til the End

Sometimes the more you hang out with someone, the more they get on your nerves. That was definitely the case after a while with me and Rodney. After years of spending more time with each other than with our own families, we simply weren't getting along like the old days. Rodney thought Abs and I had isolated him, but that was far from the truth. Abs and I were back living together and Rodney was with his wife, but in my eyes our friendship never changed. When you're close to someone, you have your ups and downs. But if you're true friends, you'll work it out, and this wasn't the first time in our friendship that we struggled with communication.

Before we were ever even in the Posse, we hadn't talked for over a year because of a drunken argument at a house party that took place back in 1995. To be completely honest, I thought I might never speak to him again. But then one night I'm out with some friends when in walks Rodney and Shane. Shane didn't even realize things had gotten so bad between us until he saw the looks on our faces. So, Shane being Shane, he sat us down and said he wasn't letting either one of us leave until we worked things out. Things between Rodney and Shane weren't great either since the release, but here was Shane, telling us that we needed to fix our shit. Here we were, two stubborn-ass guys who were both too proud to budge, but Shane just got in our faces and told us that we'd been friends for too long for this bullshit to continue. So as the liquor kept pouring and the night moved into morning we decided to keep the past in the past, and by the time we walked out of that bar you'd never even have known that we had been mad at each other. And that's just the way our relationship has been from that day forward. Sure, we know how to push each other's buttons, but at the same time we know that deep down we're still the best of friends, and that's just the way it's always going to be.

During our three-year run wrestling, we had seen the world together. Whether we were in the gym or in the ring or goofing around in whatever city we were visiting, we always knew how to have a good time.

Nothing will ever break the bond we have. There's something about what we went through together—traveling the country and not knowing what to expect next. Don't get me wrong, we got on each other's nerves from time to time, but overall there's no one else I would rather have as a partner or best friend. Rodney will always have a special place in my heart. We go back a long way and he is as genuine as they come. I really have been blessed with great friends. Shane, Rodney, and Jason Fonio, who has been a great friend since first grade, were three of the biggest influences in my life. So when I had the honor of marrying my wife, Joanna, a couple years ago, I couldn't decide on which one would be my best man. Instead, I decided to ask all three of them to be my best men. Unfortunately, Shane had a work-related commitment and couldn't attend in time. Shane not being there was a big piece missing from my wedding, along with the absence of my dad.

Rodney and I now live only a few hours away from each other. While we don't talk or see each other as much as we would like, when we do it's like we never missed a beat.

Chapter 24

Thanks for the Memories

After my release, I went back to Connecticut. The very next day I went to Titan Tower and up to Shane's office. When I walked into his office, Shane was glad to see me but had a concerned look on his face. I walked up to him and stuck out my hand. "Thank you for the best three years of my life. I can never repay you for the opportunity you gave me."

We hugged and Shane said he thought I was going to punch him. As depressed as I was for being released, my glass was half full. It was a great run and we did something that most people only dream about. If not for Shane, I wouldn't have been able to get that run.

The whole thing started as a promotion for Shane, which turned into three years. And to this day, I still reap the benefits of it. I get asked to make live appearances, be a guest on radio shows, even receive royalty checks, and people want to do business with me in my current job sometimes because they got to see me on television. So I look at it from the standpoint that the glass is always half full. I appreciate everything Shane, and the McMahon family did for me.

I still have lingering injuries to this day, but what wrestler doesn't? You can't look at an experience like that in a negative way. Every fan who watches *Monday Night Raw* fantasizes about being in that ring with the likes of Stone Cold or the Rock or Undertaker, and I got to live that fantasy. So to go to Shane and say thank you, that was the least I could do.

The Flip Side

A few years after my wrestling career was through, I started experiencing some side effects from my time in the ring. To me, this just shows how much we truly got our asses (and heads) kicked in. I'm being realistic. Sure, I loved every second I was on TV, every second I got to be Pete Gas of the Mean Street Posse, but there were negatives to the wrestling life as well, and the worst of it has to do with memory loss. For me, I just started realizing that things were getting harder and harder to remember. And it's not stuff from when I was a kid, it's more spur of the moment. If you ask me right now about something that just happened, I might not be able to figure it out. It started to concern me around 2008. I was dating a girl and brought her to meet my family at my brother's house. My niece ran up to us, and she was about seven years old, just the cutest little thing, and I went to introduce my girlfriend Natalya to her, and I was like, "Natalya, this is…" but I couldn't remember her name. My niece thought I was just playing games, but honestly, I just froze. Finally my niece goes, "Uncle Pete, you know my name is Katie." And she just laughed, but to me it was no laughing matter. Thank God she said it, because I couldn't remember my own niece's name. And then it started to happen more often, where I started to forget even some of my close friends' names. I never lost track of where I was and I never got lost driving, but to me, if you ask me something on the spot, I have a hard time remembering.

It's funny, because Shane thought I was going to punch him in the face. He said he knew how much it hurt, but that he didn't personally know how much it truly hurt to get cut. It's like your world has been taken away from you. Going in front of thousands of people and hearing them boo or cheer you is one of the greatest feelings in the world, and I get goosebumps just thinking about it. You never want that boost of adrenaline to end. The fame is great, the money is fantastic, and there's nothing like walking down the street and hearing people whisper, "Hey, that's Pete Gas." I got to experience that euphoria because of Shane and his family, so as hurt as I was, I couldn't be pissed off because without him it never would've happened in the first place. The only thing I could do is say, "Thank you," and I'm still saying thank you to this day. I told him, "If you ever need anything, I'll have my bags packed and I'll be ready to go. Whatever you want. It was the greatest experience of my life."

What's great is that our friendship and wild nights out together didn't stop just because I was no longer a part of the roster.

One weeknight in particular really stands out. It was about ten years after my release, back in 2010, and I had already gotten home from hanging out with a few friends when my phone rang. It was Shane.

"What are you doing home so early? Don't be a pussy, come back out with me." He lived in New York, but was back in Stamford celebrating Kevin Dunn's (WWE executive vice president, television production) birthday. Everyone from the office was partying down at Bennett's Steak and Fish House, so Shane thought it would be fun for me to come down, see everyone, and have a drink (or several). So I end up heading over, and as soon as I walk through the door, I see Vinnie Mac himself. He greets me with a big bear hug, and then Shane walks over and hands me a drink. I didn't want it, but then he tells me it's Louis XIII cognac. That's like $200 a drink! I was like, "Don't waste this on me," but Shane just shakes his head so what the hell, $200 down the hatch.

I walk around the party and ended up talking to John Laurinaitis, WWE's VP of talent relations (and formerly Johnny Ace). When we were talking, he started going off on how at first he hated our characters because he was stuck in Japan wrestling while us green guys who were Shane's friends were getting air time on *Raw*. But the more he watched us, the more he realized that we were getting better and better, and not only did he think we were there to stay, we grew on him to the point where he actually found us entertaining. That was great to hear, and we could've talked all night, but that's when Shane interrupted and told me he wanted me to jump in his new ride and head up to Norwalk with him to see one of his friends. The party was breaking up because, even though it was after midnight, Vince wanted to go work out. I thought he was joking, but he had a match coming up against Bret Hart and he wanted to look good and get in better shape, so he literally went from the party and drinking cognac straight to the gym to work out for a couple of hours. Crazy.

We go outside and Shane, or as I like to call him "Mr. Adrenaline Junkie," has a Ferrari 599 parked in the lot. Now, a very important thing to know about Shane is this: Shane has never bought a car that is a stock model. Everything he buys has more juice, a better engine, and a better sound system than what you'd find on the lot, and this Ferrari was no different. The thing was like a freakin' race car. Shane lives for that rush, and this Ferrari was Shane's vice at the time. We drove from Exit 8 in Stamford to exit 18 in Norwalk, a normal ride that would take the average person about eighteen minutes—only we got there in three. Three fucking minutes from Stamford to Norwalk! Shane was going about 160 miles per hour on the highway. He had the music blaring with some crazy ass techno shit at full blast, and I'm looking at the speedometer as it just kept going higher and higher.

But even at those speeds, whenever I was in the car with Shane, I never felt like my life was in danger. I've been in cars with people driving 80 and I felt unsafe, but here we were booking it down the highway at 160 and he was in complete control. But then when we got up to South Norwalk, we got lost and couldn't find where we were going. Maybe it's because when we were on the street, the speed limit was 25 and Shane was still doing over 100. Makes it difficult to see the street signs when you're flying by at those speeds.

So we're trying to figure out where we are and where we're going when out of nowhere we see a cop car start flashing its lights behind us. Shane pulls over and we hear a dog barking because on top of us being pulled over, we were now in front of a K9 unit. I'm shitting my pants thinking we're going to jail, and then Shane turns to me and says, "As soon as the cop walks up and gets to my bumper, I'm going to punch it. He'll never see us again!" I couldn't believe what he was saying. "Are you fucking crazy? Ever heard of radios?" We'd be going down for some big-time shit if he tried to run. Instead, I turn and see the cop walk up to the window and Shane turns on the charm like, "Hello officer." And the officer replied, "Shane? Gas? What are you doing here in Norwalk?" It ended up being a cop who I played softball with. He knew Shane from TV, of course, but after he bullshitted with us and told us to slow the hell down, he actually let us go.

Shane didn't get a ticket, but the cop got front row seats for *Monday Night Raw* the next night at the Mohegan Sun Arena.

Epilogue

Shane O'Mac Is Back!

February 2016

I had no idea Shane was returning to WWE. No idea. The night Shane's music hit and he danced his way back onto *Raw*, I was in shock like everyone else. What's funny is, I called him that very afternoon before the show to see what he was up to.

He said how his son had forgotten his guitar at home, so he was running to his son's school to make sure he had it for practice that day. So we shot the shit for a couple of minutes while he was driving, and when he got to his son's school, he said he had to run, but he'd talk to me soon. Later that night, there was Shane on *Raw*. I always knew that, if Shane ever came back, the place would go crazy, but I never thought they'd go *that* nuts. The roof came off the place. It was so special when he came out. It was a long time coming, and I know it meant so much to him. The WWE is in his blood. So for his sons to be able to see him in that ring was a special moment. I had the biggest grin when I was watching *Raw* that night, and I couldn't wait to give him shit the next day about not telling me.

So Tuesday comes along and I give him a call and I'm like, "You kayfabed me. You didn't tell me anything!"

Shane just laughed. "I really was dropping off my son's guitar at school. I just didn't tell you where I was going next." He told me how he headed to the airport that day, flew into Detroit, then got into a car that had dark tinted windows and rode to the arena in total secrecy. When he got out of the car, he ran to a production truck and immediately hid because he didn't want anyone to know he was there. In the Internet age, the last thing he wanted was someone to snap a photo and post it on Twitter and spoil the surprise. Shane is very big on kayfabe and not wanting to ruin the moment, and I think that's something that is missing these days. With the Internet, it seems like every big angle or return is always spoiled, so Shane went to extra lengths to make sure nobody would find out ahead of time.

Shane hid in the production truck until about ten minutes before the show started, then he started to make his way inside the arena. He said it was really weird backstage because nobody was around. Back when he was there, gorilla position was literally a 10x10 room with a folding table and a guy with a microphone. Now it's a whole different scene. He walked to gorilla, and he expected this little room, but it was this whole lounge with catering and couches and all the wrestlers were there hanging out. So he made his way to gorilla thinking he was in the clear and nobody would see him, but instead he walked right into the room where everyone was hanging out.

The entire roster was there that day, and when he walked in girls started screaming with excitement and the guys were clapping. Then, all of a sudden, Big Show picks him up and starts tossing him around like a rag doll, letting him go just long enough where he was able to walk out onto the stage and make history.

What's funny is, Shane's wife bought GoPro cameras and placed them in her house so when Shane's sons were watching the show, they had no idea their dad was going to be on. She had her cell phone and started filming right before his music hit, and their reaction was priceless. Shane was telling me the story, and it sounded like he was getting choked up, and even I started getting a little choked up as well just knowing how special the business and his family are to him. I don't think this is something Shane has ever gotten out of his system. He had always wanted to come back, and now he was back—bigger and better than ever.

As soon as his music hit, that's when my phone and iPad started blowing up with messages from all over the world. I got a big rush of Twitter followers and text messages and Facebook friend requests. Everyone was hitting me up and tagging me in posts saying that if Shane's back, does that means he's bringing the Mean Street Posse back with him?

Of course, the thing to me was, I couldn't let this all get to my head because I had no idea if I would be asked to come back with him or not. And the more hype Shane brought to *Raw*, the more calls I started getting from guys I used to work with in the business. They were all wondering if I was going back. Did I need to go sweater shopping?

One night after *Raw* I received a text from Matt Bloom (Prince Albert) asking me if I saw a Last Ride and Chokeslam in my future. I laughed and told him that I prayed to God every night that it happens. Next thing I know, I'm getting all of these media requests. I'm talking to *Rolling Stone* about Shane's return, I'm being asked to talk on all of these podcasts, and everyone wants to know if I'm coming back. To top it off, I was filming for the *Edge and Christian Show*, and when I got there, not only were Edge and Christian asking me about it, so were all of the WWE's production people.

Everyone was saying, "Shane's back, he's got to bring you back." You try to block it out, but it's hard not to think something might happen when everyone around you tells you so. To be honest, it's a rush, and to think that you could end up being part of a match at WrestleMania against the Undertaker, it's something that really gets your heart pumping. I allowed it to get in my head for a little bit, unfortunately, but it obviously didn't end up happening. There was no Posse on TV, but that doesn't mean I wasn't still going to support my boy. When I saw Vince make the stipulation that Shane's match with Taker was going to be a "Hell in a Cell" match, I turned to my wife on the couch and said, "He's gonna jump off that thing!" I knew if there was one thing I needed to do, it was to be in Dallas for his match. I told Shane that I wanted to be there for him, and he was thrilled.

He ended up hooking me up with tickets to the Hall of Fame, NXT, and WrestleMania, not to mention passes to the pre- and post-parties. Shane has always been a generous guy and does whatever he can for his friends, so even if I couldn't be out there in the match, it ended up being an amazing experience.

Shane later told me that he actually knew he was coming back to face the Undertaker for about four months before he showed up on *Raw*, so he had been training hard to get his body ready for the event. He had been working with Tommy Dreamer in the ring, as well as MMA training, and had been, well, acting like Shane, who always has to be the best at anything and everything he puts his mind to. And it's funny because the Monday night before WrestleMania, he dropped the elbow on Taker, then as he stumbled away, used his shirt to wipe his face and, when he lifted his shirt, it showed his washboard abs. I called Shane and was like, "Not to sound like a weirdo, but what's up with your stomach, bro?" I couldn't believe it. He laughed about it, but he had gotten into ridiculous shape. Knowing how he is, I knew when I saw his body and how he had been working out, he wasn't just showing up to Mania to be on the show—he was showing up to steal the show. Here he is, a forty-six-year-old who hasn't wrestled in years, but he wanted to prove that he's still the larger-than-life athlete he was when he first climbed the top of the Titantron to drop an elbow on the Big Show back in the day. Shane is about making moments, making memories, and that's exactly what he did in Dallas.

My wife and I left to fly down to Dallas on Friday, and as I packed my suitcase, there's an old rule that states: Always pack your gear. You never know when you'll get the call, so I packed a sweater vest, a white t-shirt, and a pair of black shoes (better safe than sorry, right?). The last thing I'd want to have happen is for Shane to call me at the last second and tell me they wanted to use me, and for me not to have my sweater vest. So I was ready for anything, as always.

So arrived Friday morning and ended up spending the day in downtown Dallas before heading to the NXT show that evening.

And while we were walking around, I couldn't believe how big the WrestleMania Axxess fan fest was. The thing was enormous. Anything and everything you ever wanted from a wrestling event was there. Guys from NXT were taking pictures and signing autographs, and the WWE shop they had on site was so enormous and with merchandise from just about every superstar past or present that you could think of, all I kept thinking was, *Cha-ching!* The amount of money people were spending on shirts and posters and toys was mind-blowing. If you were a wrestling fan, this was definitely the place to be, and I had never seen anything like it before. My wife and I walked over to the NXT show, and it was in this small, hot arena packed from end to end with rabid NXT fans. It reminded me a lot of ECW and how passionate the crowd was back in Philadelphia. That's how passionate these NXT fans are, and this was one of the loudest shows I have ever been to in my life.

My party days aren't what they used to be. The show started late and I remember telling my wife how exhausted I was going to be by the time it was over. But once it started, and the energy in that building was so amazing, I was pumped up beyond belief watching these incredible matches. The wrestlers of NXT brought it hard, and it was simply mind-blowing that this was supposed to be developmental wrestling. They wanted to prove what they could do in front of this WrestleMania crowd and, oh my God, compared to the developmental days in Memphis, this was a whole new ballgame. In my opinion, these NXT performers are so great that any one of them could be called up and be a huge star on the main show. From their promos to their in-ring work, everything about it was sharp and professional.

What I really enjoyed about the show, though, was sitting back and watching Shane's boys and their excitement level for everything going on around them. Knowing how this weekend was all about Shane's family and his legacy and what the WWE meant to them, watching the boys and their reactions to all of these matches live was really heartwarming. They were sitting in the first couple of rows, and they look so much like Shane, in my eyes, and were jumping around having an absolute blast.

The NXT matches were awesomely insane, especially when Samoa Joe was out there bleeding so badly that they actually had to stop the match. It actually made me laugh because they would've never stopped a match for blood back in the Attitude Era. At WrestleMania 2000, I bled all over the place after being hit with those cookie sheets. I was bleeding like a stuck pig. I had the crimson mask. Imagine stopping the hardcore matches because of blood?! But this is a good thing, as it shows how they're looking out more for the safety of the performers, not to mention attempting to make the show more family friendly.

Shane's boys were lucky, though, because during that match they were hanging over the rail in the front row, but decided to sit back for just a few seconds—and as soon as they sat back in their seats, Joe torpedoed himself through the second and third ropes and came flying right into the railing where they had just been standing. He crashed hard into the guard rail, and it was the old school guard rail that had movement to it, so it's a lucky thing they were sitting back or they would've gotten nailed by Joe and that railing.

The whole NXT show had a great vibe to it—not just inside the ring, but throughout the arena. There were so many people at that show, from X-Pac to Scott Hall to the McMahon family. Everyone was out there to show their support to NXT and, boy, did they put on a show.

* * *

Saturday night was the Hall of Fame. That was a really fun night that really brought back a lot of memories. And Shane, as always, made sure my wife and I were really taken care of.

You see, everything Shane does is first-class, can't-be-done-better type of event. For example, we got to the room in Dallas and waiting for us was a basket that Shane and Marissa had sent that had WrestleMania t-shirts, hats, candy, cookies, and a WrestleMania program. Then, on Saturday evening, they had a car service pick us up and take us to the Fairmont hotel, as WWE had bus service for everyone on their "friends and family" list from the Fairmont to the Hall of Fame arena.

There were like four or five buses, and Terri Runnels, who used to be the Mean Street Posse's manager back in the day (for about a month), was sitting in front of us. She is really one of the sweetest ladies I've ever met, and the way she greeted us, my wife couldn't believe not only how nice she was, but how well all the wrestlers and people involved in the business treated their peers. The friendship among wrestlers is so much stronger than any other friendship I've ever had or seen, and I think it's because you're putting your lives on the line together; your life is in their hands and their life is in yours when you're in the ring performing and it creates this bond and respect that's undeniable. As someone who was and always will be a fan, riding that bus really was special. When you look around, you saw everyone from Jake "The Snake" Roberts to Sheamus to the Usos to Natalya to a bunch of the other divas. And as we rode to the event, everyone was so sweet introducing themselves to my wife and myself and, like I said, the amount of respect is amazing. That was the biggest thing to my wife, and she's still blown away by how every wrestler would come up and talk to us and show us respect. Meanwhile if we walk down the block by our house, our own neighbors are probably more likely to snub us than to simply say hi. It's just a completely different world.

Eventually, the bus took us down to the arena, and I remember thinking to myself that everyone was so respectful now and how different it was when we Rodney and I first walked in the arena for our first live event as Shane's friends . . . who just so happened to now be starring on TV. But the respect factor years later is so much greater than it was in the beginning. It's the whole thing about respecting your elders. These younger wrestlers knew who I was, they knew I was there on *Raw* before them, and they actually acted excited to meet me and my wife.

When we got to the arena, there were various places in the back to take pictures, and there was even a red carpet for the ultimate photo op. Terri kept bugging me to walk the red carpet, but I knew the night wasn't about me, so my wife and I walked off to the side and talked to some people like *SmackDown* announcer Mauro Ranallo and old-school jobber turned backstage agent, the Brooklyn Brawler. I talked to Brawler for about a half hour and it was so much fun catching up. Brawler was almost as big of a jobber as the Posse, but he has so much respect in the business for all the years he's put in.

* * *

I still hadn't seen Shane yet and didn't see him throughout the show, but when the ceremony was over we lined back up to return to the hotel on the bus. Then all of a sudden I looked up and could see Shane about 15 yards away from us back by the door. I waited for the noise level to die down then I shouted out a nickname I had for him back from Spanish class, and his head snapped back and he pointed for me to come backstage. It was so good to catch up and give him a hug. I hadn't seen him physically for about a year, so it was great because my wife got to meet Shane's wife, Marissa, and we all had a long talk. Shane and I took a really nice picture backstage and he told us that he was hoping to see us at the after-party once WrestleMania was over. I knew all along that he was going to do something stupid during the match: and by stupid, I mean dangerous. So I told him, "Good luck in your match. I'm looking forward to seeing what happens." He seemed blown away that I wanted to come to WrestleMania to see him, and he kept telling me how much it meant that I had made it to Dallas, but I just told him, "Why wouldn't I come see you? This is a big deal." He was really, really grateful, but I wouldn't have missed it for the world.

* * *

The next day was Mania, and we took a bus they had reserved for family and guests of the talent to the big show. We drove down to AT&T Stadium and I couldn't get over the size of Jerry's World. In fact, they actually shut down the highway and all the buses had a police escort the entire way.

After grabbing a bite to eat, we made our way down to the seats, which were fourth-row lined up with the center of the ring (thanks, Shane!). Amazing. I just kept shaking my head and laughing. Everyone around us was family, friends, and celebrities. A lot of the NXT guys were standing 10 to 15 feet behind us. I headed to the back and saw RVD standing at the bar, doing his patented thumb-point for everyone while drinking his beer.

I headed over to the bathroom, and just as I'm about to walk in, walking out was the one and only Pat Patterson.

I said, "Hey Pat," and he stopped and looked at me funny. He totally didn't remember me at first.

"Pat, don't you recognize me?" And he looks at me all fuzzy again and kind of tilts his head in a strange position. I don't know, maybe it was the beer, but finally it clicks and he goes, "The Posse!" So I brought him over to the bar and I ordered him a drink for old times while we shared a few laughs.

Eventually, I went back to my seat because Shane's match was coming up. I could've stayed and caught up with old friends all night if I wanted, but I knew I had to get back and see what Shane was going to try and pull off against Taker. I just didn't know how far he'd go to make sure he had that "moment."

When Shane's music hit, he came down and did his dance thing, then stopped and headed to the back for a second. All of a sudden, while I'm sitting there watching, my phone starts blowing up with messages again, as people thought for sure the Mean Street Posse was going to come out with him.

But this year, it was Shane's new posse: his sons. It was so cool to see Shane's boys go out there and ham it up in front of the live crowd. That was a moment their family will never forget (and I'm sure gets played on YouTube at the McMahon residence on a non-stop loop). They were able go out there and walk that ramp like their father and grandfather before them, and they looked like they were having the time of their young lives. It couldn't help bring a tear to your eye, especially when you consider how much Shane loves both the business and his boys. Shane hadn't been seen on *Raw* for like seven years, and now he was not only back, but had his boys as part of his return to WrestleMania. This, to me, was truly special.

Once they made their way down to ringside, the boys found their way over the barricade, and Shane entered the Hell in a Cell. We made eye contact and I gave him a Mean Street Posse chest pound just like the old days. He gave me a head nod to acknowledge it, and I immediately thought to myself: *I know this guy is going to the top of the cage. His whole life has been about jumping off of the highest thing possible, so there was no way he wasn't going up there.* He's always been just crazy enough to jump off the top of the Cell, and as the match progressed and he hit his signature moves, I was waiting to see how they were going to make their way out of the cage and climb to the top.

As soon as Shane found those bolt cutters, I turned to my wife and said, "He's going to jump!" He had Taker laid out on the table and started to climb. I really didn't want him to do it. I knew he was going to do it, but I was seriously worried for him. Sure, it wasn't as high as the dam he jumped off of in high school, but he also wasn't landing in water. I knew there was an airbag underneath that table, but god forbid: what if something happened? And when he jumped, if you were in the arena, it seemed like it was happening in super speed. You could see the velocity pick up as he fell, and all I could think was, *He's nuts. He's absolutely nuts!* He was picking up more and more speed as he was coming down until the impact of the table made a sickening thud.

The thing is, when you jump off the top rope and land on the announcer's table, you don't have the ability to pick up too much speed. But when he fell straight down off the cage, he was really moving, and that's one thing that I'm not sure was picked up on TV. He hit that table so solid.

After the match, my wife turned to me and asked if I was all right. "You look so worried." But I just wanted to make sure he was OK. It really was a scary fall, and when the show ended, I was still extremely concerned for Shane. The one thing that made me think he wasn't hurt was the reaction from Linda, his mom, as she was still sitting in the front row after his match ended. If something was wrong, there's no way she'd sit there for the rest of the show.

After Mania we ended up back at the hotel, and it was time for the after party. This was probably my favorite part of the entire weekend. When Shane told me that my wife and I were invited to the after-party, I was really excited because I knew the entire roster would be there. And it's not like meeting these guys at an autograph signing or something like that. You were there as one of their peers, and they were all really inviting and friendly. I got to catch up with Zack Ryder and Emma for a bit, then I got to talk NXT with Matt Bloom and Steven Regal. Being able to catch up with them brought back so many memories and stories. They were bringing up funny things we did that I hadn't thought about in over a decade. We had a lot of laughs. My wife told me, "The look on your face was unbelievable. You lit up, they lit up, and I've never seen you like this before."

One of the biggest reactions I got that night was from Chris Jericho. He was talking to Christian, and I went up and tapped him on the shoulder, and when he turned around, he had a huge smile on his face and gave me the biggest hug of the night. It was so great to see a guy like that—a guy who you have so much respect for—and to see his reaction to seeing me was priceless. Spending time with those guys, and getting to meet some of the newer guys like Xavier Woods from the New Day, was just incredible. Xavier was there with his wife and Kofi Kingston and his wife, and Xavier sees me and he's waving me over like, "Pete Gas from the Mean Street Posse!" He was so funny. The admiration from everybody was unbelievable, and it was all mutual. I don't know how to explain it, but it's just something about being a part of the business. I'm a generation away from Xavier Woods, but these guys are just respectful as hell about the business, which continues to blow my mind.

It was getting late. It was about 3:30 a.m. EST, which is usually the time I usually get *up* for work, so I turn to my wife and ask if she's ready to go. I was disappointed Shane never made it to the party, but I couldn't wait much longer.

Finally we made our way out of the hotel ballroom, and on our way out we see the Big Show. I introduced him to my wife, and the thing about the Big Show is that he is a great big teddy bear. He's just a great guy, and shaking his hand is like shaking a catcher's mitt, so I was excited to introduce him to my wife. After we saw Big Show, we ended up running into Kane and it was great to talk to him a little bit (and bust his balls about dominoes!).

Then just as we were leaving Kane, we saw X-Pac, and it's funny because we were trying to leave, but everywhere you looked was someone you wanted to talk to, and the night just kept getting later and later.

We finally made our way out of the party, and as we go down the escalator I look into the lobby and there's Shane talking to Stone Cold Steve Austin and the Nature Boy himself, Ric Flair. Shane's boys are there with him along with his wife, Marissa, and when I see Shane, he was seriously moving like some sort of hunch-back snail. Dude was definitely feeling that fall from the cage. I asked him, "How are you feeling?" He turned his whole body toward me and smirked and said, "I'm wonderful, can't you tell?" I laughed because I didn't know how he was feeling, but at the same time I was glad I didn't know because from the way he was moving he didn't seem that great. We talked for a little bit and I told him, "I'd hug you, but I'm afraid I'd break whatever is left of you." He just started laughing. I was glad to see he was up and moving because, like I said, that was one of the scariest falls in the history of this business. What still blows me away to this day is that he was so appreciative of me coming to Dallas. But like I told him, I wouldn't have missed it for the world. Part of me wishes he would've asked me to be involved in the match, but it was still an honor just to be a part of this major event as his friend. It was special just knowing how important the whole event meant to him now that he was back in the family business. Then again, if Shane ever invites me out to another big match, I just hope he knows one thing: I'm packing my sweater vest.

I can already imagine how the phone call would go: "Hey Pete, so how much vacation time do you have . . . ?"

As much as you need, Shane. As much as you need.

Acknowledgments

This book could not have been written without help from many special people. Through it all, my experiences and interactions with these people have molded me into who I am today.

First off, a huge thank you to Jon Robinson. Without you, my dream would never have become a reality. You did an amazing job and made writing this book together a great experience. Plus, I also made a good friend in the process.

Thank you to all my childhood friends who were there from day one in the neighborhood. Since grade school you guys have been there for me. Bobby Capalbo and Vinny Insigna have seen it all.

Jason Fronio, one of my best friends and classmate from first grade through college, you and your family are my second family. Jason's dad Artie gave us wisdom in his own special way over the years and that will last a lifetime. His outlook and theories could be the reason why we look at life the way we do.

My high school coaches Mike Ornato and Rocky DeCarlo. Two of the best coaches I ever had. They motivated me to be the best I can be and taught me discipline that has stayed with me ever since. Thank you both.

My UConn Football teammates and brothers. You guys were there through the good times and the bad. Rob Belcuore and Brian Kozlowski, we shared many meals and laughs. My mom still talks about how many ravioli she made that day we left for training camp.

Rick Jackson, Mark Chapman, Mark Didio, and Vinny Marino. Friends and roommates that grew up together. You guys were there for me through a very tough time in my life. Thank you.

To the rest of my college teammates throughout my time at the University of Connecticut I will never forget the standing ovation you gave me running onto the practice field less than 48 hours after thumb surgery. I was blessed to get to play alongside all of you.

Former head coach Tom Jackson. No one had a bigger influence on my life in college than you. You were tough, yet still a player's coach. Your comments on the sidelines still bring laughs to us today. Most importantly, I left college a man because of you.

Along the way I made great friends who played a part in my development and should be acknowledged. John Bosco, Dave Corbo, Chris Silver, Ben Rossi, Curtis Vaden, Bob Deregibus, Rob and Kathleen Romano, Chris Gilman, Aaron and Justin Valenti, Kris O'Hara, George Legierse, Tim Daly, and Doug Roina.

Chris "Skip" Bossone, thank you for being more than my boss. You have been a friend and brother. My respect for you is much greater than you realize.

To my wrestling trainers. A special thanks to Dr. Tom Pritchard, my first trainer. I hope all those potatoes I gave you have healed by now. Thank you for having patience with us.

Michael P. S. Hayes, Terry Taylor, Bruce Pritchard and Jack Lanza, Vince Russo, Ed Ferrara, and Tommy Blancha, you were all a huge influence on me when we first started. Thank you.

Tony Garea, your sayings will last a lifetime. The title of this book was inspired because of you. I will also always remember, "Hey kid . . . I've seen your work. Don't quit your day job." Thank you, Tony.

Steven Regal, Robby Brookside, Jim Neidhart, Bobby Eaton, Terry Golden, Savio Vega, Dutch Mantel, Jerry Lawler, and Tracey Smothers. I learned so much from all of you. My experiences and lessons in Memphis and Puerto Rico stick with me today.

My Memphis family, a group that truly grew up together in so many ways. Ron Killings, Brian Kendrick, Bryan Danielson, Murray Happer, Mike Howell, Lisa Marie Varon, Charlie Haas, Kevin Fertig, Kevin Kelly, Stacey Carter, Cyndi Lynch, and to the family members who have passed. Lance Cade, Russ Haas and Steve Bradley. Rest in peace, we miss you.

To the entire roster during the Attitude Era. There are so many of you and I thank you all for accepting me into your family. Sean Morley, Bob Holly, Sean Waltman, Brian James, Kip Sopp, Matt Bloom, Paul Levesque, Tommy Dreamer, Trish Stratus, Amy Dumas, Bubba and Devon, D-Lo and Chaz Warrington, Ron Simmons, John Layfield, Charles Wright, Paul Wight, Dwayne Johnson, Steve Williams, Jim Ross, Adam Copeland, Jay Reso, Matt and Jeff Hardy, John Cena, Kurt Angle,

Glen Jacobs, and Mark Calloway. You guys helped in so many facets of the business and made me a better performer. It was an honor and pleasure, and your hard work dedication, and respect for the business was contagious.

Jason Ahrndt, you were more than a mentor and partner. You're family. We drove all over the country and shared some great memories. Having you as a partner was one of the many highlights of my career.

Rod Leinhardt, we did it! We had zero experience and were thrown in the ring with the best in the business and held our own. We made the most of our opportunity and getting to do that with you made it all the more special. This experience made us even closer friends, and remember that you can always count on me.

Vince, Linda, and Stephanie McMahon: thank you for everything. You gave me opportunities and experiences that I wouldn't have had without your help. Words cannot describe the respect and admiration I have for you all. Since I was a kid coming to your house, you have always treated me like family and I appreciate that, when I worked for you, I was treated like anyone else. I wouldn't have wanted it any other way.

Shane-O Mac, my friend since high school, you have given me a gift in which I can never repay. The opportunity you provided made a bigger impact in my life than anyone could have realized even to this day. More importantly, it's your friendship that has meant the most. You have been there for me in countless good times and bad.

My in-laws, Jack and Donna Dinolfo. You have accepted me into your family and could not treat me any better.

My brother Dan and Kelly Gasparino. Thank you for the support and inspiration over the years. Dan, you will always be a motivator for me. Your success in life as an athlete, father, and career man inspires me to emulate your success.

My brother Mike and Ruth Gasparino. Ruth, you have been like a sister to me since I can remember, and your mom was like a second mother to me. Thank you for the support over the years. Mike, you have been my measuring stick my entire life. You've always been the one I've looked up to. Thank you for all your help growing up and being there for me whenever I needed it. Your calls during my time in wrestling really inspired me to work even harder.

My sister Patti and Mark O'Gorman. Patti, you have always been there for me and throughout the years and understand me better than anyone. Because we are closer in age I'll always protective of my little sister. Mark, you have been like a brother to me. Thanks for your support over the years.

My nieces and nephews: Michael, Christy, Paige, Brynn, Tommy, Maggie, Katie, and Jack. You all mean the world to me and I love you all.

My mother, Patricia. You are the glue that holds it all together and the strongest person I know. When we lost dad, you stepped up and always seemed to have things under control. Thank you for being there for me. I love you.

The original Pete Gas. He was a man of few words unless you knew him. He was tough on us for the right reasons and taught me to think about why I do things before doing them. Not to say I always do that, but in certain aspects of my life I do.

Last but not least, Joanna, my beautiful wife and the best thing that's ever happened to me. You are the one who supported and gave me the inspiration to chase this dream. Without your help, this book would never have been written. I love you.